Elite • 252

Roman Mail and Scale Armour

M.C. BISHOP

ILLUSTRATED BY GIUSEPPE RAVA
Series editors Martin Windrow & Nick Reynolds

OSPREY PUBLISHING
Bloomsbury Publishing Plc
Kemp House, Chawley Park, Cumnor Hill, Oxford OX2 9PH, UK
29 Earlsfort Terrace, Dublin 2, Ireland
1385 Broadway, 5th Floor, New York, NY 10018, USA
E-mail: info@ospreypublishing.com
www.ospreypublishing.com

OSPREY is a trademark of Osprey Publishing Ltd

First published in Great Britain in 2023

A catalogue record for this book is available from the British Library.

ISBN: PB 9781472851703; eBook 9781472851710;
ePDF 9781472851697; XML 9781472851680

23 24 25 26 27   10 9 8 7 6 5 4 3 2 1

Index by Rob Munro
Typeset by PDQ Digital Media Solutions, Bungay, UK
Printed and bound in India by Replika Press Private Ltd.

Osprey Publishing supports the Woodland Trust, the UK's leading woodland conservation charity.

To find out more about our authors and books visit **www.ospreypublishing.com**. Here you will find extracts, author interviews, details of forthcoming events and the option to sign up for our newsletter.

Acknowledgements

As was the case for the companion volume to this (Elite 247 *Roman Plate Armour*), I am grateful to a number of people for their kind assistance in the preparation of this work. Barbara Birley was good enough to provide an image of the wire-drawing plate from Vindolanda. Alex Croom kindly supplied photographs of the South Shields mail. Once again, Holger von Grawert helped with the sourcing of images. Thanks are due to Prof Simon James for allowing me to use his images of the Dura-Europos 'lamellar' cuisses, as well as Andreas Pangerl, who permitted me to reproduce his photographs of armour and fittings from Carnuntum and Vindonissa. I am grateful to Dr Katia Schörle and Victoria Delgado of the Musée d'Art Classique de Mougins for facilitating the use of the image of the helmet with the scale aventail, while Dr Martijn Wijnhoven was kind enough to allow me to reproduce his photographs and explanatory diagram of the Bertoldsheim cuirass. Dr David Sim not only generously provided the weight of his reconstruction of the Carlisle scale armour, but I have also benefited over the years from many conversations with him on the production and use of mail and scale armour, as I have with the late (and much missed) Peter Connolly. Finally, as is so often the case, my friend and colleague Dr Jon Coulston allowed me to use some of his huge range of images, for which I thank him, as well as for agreeing to read and comment upon an early draft of this text. All errors and infelicities that remain are, sadly, my own fault.

Artist's note

Readers may care to note that the original paintings from which the colour plates in this book were prepared are available for private sale. All reproduction copyright whatsoever is retained by the publishers. All enquiries should be addressed to:

info@g-rava.com

The publishers regret that they can enter into no correspondence upon this matter.

Back-cover illustration: Tombstone of the auxiliary cavalryman C. Romanius Capito from Mainz-Zahlbach showing his mail shirt with shoulder doubling and breast fastening hook but no surface detail on the armour. The indication of mail would have been added in paint. (Photo © M.C. Bishop)

Title-page illustration: Mail indicated with light chiselling on the surface of the armour of an auxiliary soldier on a cast of Trajan's Column, made in the 19th century and now in the Museo della Civiltà Romana in the Esposizione Universale Roma business district of Rome. The detail on the original sculpture has now largely been eroded away by the combined effects of weathering and pollution. (Photo © M.C. Bishop)

CONTENTS

ROMAN MAIL AND SCALE ARMOUR

INTRODUCTION

Roman plate armour may well be one of the most easily recognizable cultural identifiers of any of the peoples in the ancient world, but it can plausibly be argued that it was less significant militarily than both mail and scale armour. For the sculptors of Trajan's Column in Rome, however, mail was the armour of the auxiliary infantry and cavalry, while scale belonged to exotic troops and foes. By contrast, the artists who produced the sculpted panels or metopes of the Tropaeum Traiani monument at Adamclisi (Romania) – probably military personnel, unlike the metropolitan sculptors – used mail and scale for all Roman troops and ignored segmental body armour. Given that both monuments supposedly depict the same conflict, the Emperor Trajan's (r. AD 98–117) two Dacian Wars of AD 101–02 and AD 105–06, there is clearly a problem in taking one of them at face value. Fortunately, provincial sculpture provides a more plausible representation of the types of armour in use, which can be verified from the archaeological record.

Dominate soldiers on the Vatican Chiaramonti relief showing mail (left) and scale (right) body armour. (Drawing © M.C. Bishop)

Origins

Neither mail nor scale is Roman in origin. Mail originated with the pre-Roman Iron Age peoples of northern Europe (often identified with the vague term 'Celts') and was perhaps a natural development from the new-found mastery of ferrous technology in the 1st millennium BC. Early examples of mail found at Tiefenau (Switzerland) and Ciumeşti (Romania) were in fact made entirely from ferrous wire with butted ends, but this raises the question (ultimately unanswerable) of whether this was intended for actual use in combat or whether, since the former was found in a watery context, it was ritual in purpose.

Terminology

For the purposes of this volume, the tautological 'chain mail' will be avoided in favour of just 'mail', following the reasoning of Kelly and Schwabe (1931: 48). The modern English word 'mail' derives from the French *maille*, which in turn comes from the Latin *macula*, meaning a mesh, although this was not the term used by the Romans for mail armour. It is notable that Polybios used the Greek adjective ἁλυσιδωτός ('chain-like'; see p. 16), so it is conceivable that this lies at the root of the English penchant for 'chain mail'.

Painted Hellenistic funerary stele from Saida depicting Salmamodes of Adada wearing mail armour. (PHAS/Universal Images Group via Getty Images)

The Romans termed all forms of body armour '*lorica*', the origin of the word being explained by Varro, as well as the later broadening of its compass to include mail: '*Lorica*, because they made chest armour from strips (*lora*) of rawhide; later, the Gallic iron defence was included under this term, a tunic made of iron rings' (Varro, *de Lingua Latina* 5.116). The English language has a number of words for the defence as a whole, the antiquated 'hauberk' (Frankish in origin as *halsberg*, ultimately *hauberk* in Middle English) being favoured by some, while 'shirt' is perhaps more common. 'Cuirass' is equally dated but, since it – like *lorica* – reflected (rightly or wrongly) a perceived leather origin for body armour, is also regularly used.

It is now generally assumed that the noun *lorica* was qualified with an adjective, '*hamata*' for mail and '*squamata*' for scale, with the former ('hooked') derived from *hama* (hooks) and the latter (literally 'scaly') from *squamae* (scales, like those of a fish). This is certainly the impression left by the post-Roman etymologist Isidore of Seville, writing in the 6th/7th centuries AD: 'On armour (*loricae*). Armour (*lorica*) is so called because it lacks leather straps (*lorum*); for it only comprises iron rings. Scale (*squama*) is iron armour with plates of iron or bronze joined in the manner of fish scales, and named from its shiny similarity to scales. Moreover the armour is both polished and covered by a goat-skin garment (*cilicium*)' (Isidore, *Etym*. 18.13.1–2, tr. the author). Isidore's last comment may be a misunderstanding of the padded garment (or 'arming doublet'; see p. 57) worn under the armour or, alternatively, an indication that a garment was worn over a *lorica*, as Robinson (1975: Pls 243–44) suggested. Robinson's supposed representational evidence for this, however, is at best debatable (see p. 57).

Nevertheless, no Roman-era writer actually used the terms '*lorica hamata*' or '*lorica squamata*', although they are found (at the same time as

Roman soldiers wearing both mail and scale armour on the Marcus Column, the mail being indicated by means of a series of drilled holes. (Photo © M.C. Bishop)

'lorica segmentata'; Bishop 2022: 10) in the 1596 work *de Militia Romana* by Just Lips (aka Iustus Lipsius) as *lorica hamata* and *lorica squamae* (*sic*), which constitutes the first serious discussion in the modern era of the terminology employed by the Romans for these types of armour:

Lorica hamata
'*Loricae* containing hooks.' Greek θώρακας ἁλυσιδωτούς [*thōrakas halusidōtous*], for which the term would be *lorica catenata*: but Latin speakers, like me, said this. I believe, because rings and chains are linked, they referred to the form of halved hooks: or because they also made chains from hooks? Sidonius is seen to say this:
'– and she wore no / Body armour woven from a ring held together with hooks' [*Carmina* 321–2]
Although you can translate it even for the former sense. *Lorica hamata* was changed by an old translator of the Bible, when the Greek is θώρακας ἁλυσιδωτοὺς: and hooks or chains are the rule here and there. In Virgil:
'The breastplate, intertwined with hooks of triple gold.' [*Aeneid* 3.259–60]
In Lucan: 'which twisted heavy *lorica catena* / He faces.' [*Pharsalia* 7.498–9]
In Statius: 'breastplate of several repeated thin chains.' [*Thebaid* 12.775] (Lipsius 1630: 129 – Liber III Dialog. vi, tr. author)

On the subject of scale, Just Lips wrote:

Lorica squamae
The Greeks call them φολιδωτοὺς [*pholidōtous*] or λεπιδωτοὺς [*lepidōtous*], from the scales of fish or serpents. Thus Plutarch

---

A | **ANATOMY OF MAIL AND SCALE**
This plate depicts eight types of mail and scale defence worn by Roman soldiers from the 2nd century BC through to the 4th century AD: (**1**) a mail shirt with shoulder doubling, edged throughout in leather, and fastened at the breast with a hinged pair of S-shaped hooks; (**2**) a one-piece mail shirt with short sleeves; (**3**) a one-piece mail shirt with a pair of embossed breast fastening plates; (**4**) a one-piece mail shirt with long sleeves; (**5**) a scale shirt with shoulder doubling fastened at the breast with a hinged pair of S-shaped hooks; (**6**) a scale shirt with a shoulder cape; (**7**) a scale shirt with a pair of embossed breast fastening plates; and (**8**) hybrid armour, with fine scale attached to fine mail. Archaeological finds demonstrate how many variables there were in implementing both mail (ring size, wire diameter) and scale (size and number of scales, thickness and type of metal employed) armour, affecting both the weight and protection offered (all Roman armour having to compromise between these two factors). Thus, any answers to questions such as 'how heavy was a mail shirt?' and 'how many scales did *lorica squamata* contain?' can only ever be approximated for particular sets of armour, never for types as a whole.

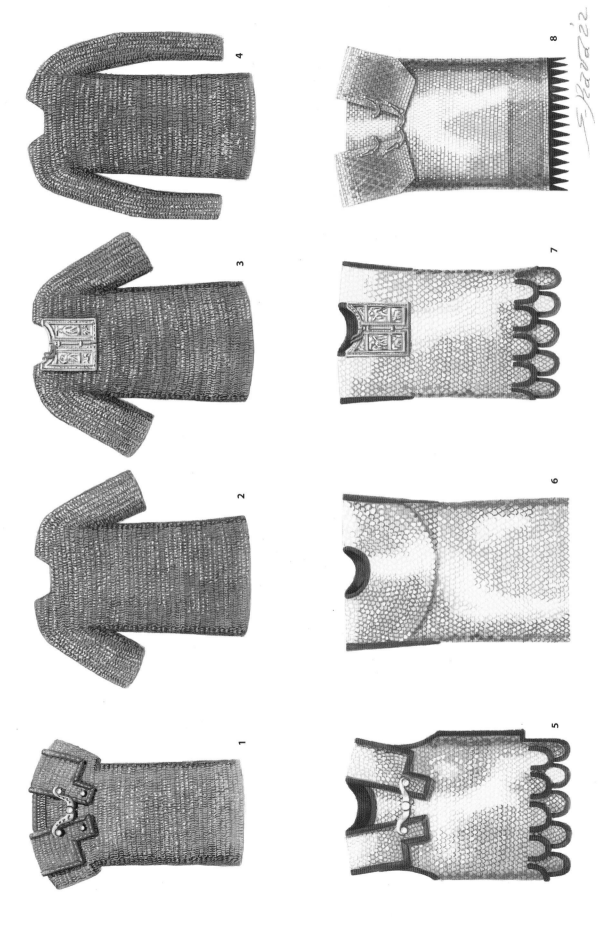

An *adlocutio* (an address by the emperor) scene on a relief panel on the Arch of Constantine, generally held to come from a monument of Marcus Aurelius whose figure has been modified to depict the emperor Constantine (r. AD 306–37). This scene shows both mail and scale armour, the former in a highly stylized form as a grid of incised lines and drilled holes. (Photo © M.C. Bishop)

writes that Lucullus, on the very day in which he fought against Tigranes, had to be clothed in θώρακα σιδηροῦν φολιδωτὸν [*thōraka sidēroun pholidōton: Lucullus* 28]: armour of iron scales. And Dio Cassius, emperor Macrinus took from the Praetorians τοὺς θώρακας τοὺς λεπιδωτοὺς [*tous thorakas tous lepidotous: Roman History* 79.37], scale breastplates: and from these examples, he has clearly distinguished himself. I am stating that these consisted of both hooks and solid plates. From Silius, on the arming of the consul Flaminius:

'Then he put on his breastplate; its twisted links were embossed with plates wrought of hard steel mingled with gold.' [*Punica* 5.140–41]
(Lipsius 1630: 129 – Liber III Dialog. vi, tr. author)

In this Just Lips was anticipating discussions that would be had many years later on the subject of hybrid mail and scale armour (see p. 34).

Under the Dominate, the term *cataphracta/catafracta* seems to have been used synonymously with *lorica*, doubtless because cataphracts (armoured cavalry) began to be adopted in the early 2nd century AD by the Roman Army and, by association, came to be synonymous with body armour. The term is found in Vegetius' eclectic *De Re Militari* (e.g. DRM 1.16, 1.20, 2.14–16, 3.23). This term is undoubtedly ambiguous in its application and may reflect the epitomator's use of multiple sources to compile his works (initially one book, later expended to four). This can be contrasted with the *Notitia Dignitatum*, in which workshops (*fabricae*) for both *loricae* (ND Occ. 9) and *clibanaria* (ND Occ. 9.31 and Or. 11; presumably where the accoutrements of the heavily armoured cavalry known as *clibanarii* were manufactured) are to be found.

MAIL ARMOUR

Mail was a ubiquitous form of body armour throughout the Roman period, but it is almost certainly under-represented in the archaeological record, to judge from the available representational sources. *Lorica segmentata*, beloved of the sculptors of the friezes on both Trajan's Column and the Marcus Column, the latter erected to commemorate the emperor Marcus Aurelius' (r. AD 161–80) Marcomannic Wars (AD 166–80), seems to have been much more vulnerable to attrition than mail, hence the former found its way into the ground much more readily than the latter and its copper-alloy fittings are easily identified.

Sculptural evidence plays an important role in understanding the adoption and development of mail in the Roman world, but interpreting it is not straightforward. As Robinson pointed out, there was a variety of ways of depicting mail, ranging from detailed carving of rings, through fairly crude drilling and chiselling, to simply adding detail in paint, often on a gesso base. The more detailed representations can be found on monumental sculpture, such as a Hellenistic frieze from the Sanctuary of Athena Polias at Pergamon (Turkey) and the Roman-era statue of a man from Vachères (France). Chiselling was used on the four marble panels that decorated the base of the so-called Altar of Domitius Ahenobarbus (also known as the Census Relief) in Rome and on Trajan's Column, while paint on gesso seems to have been favoured for Roman military tombstones such as the centurion M. Favonius Facilis from Colchester (England) and the legionary C. Valerius Crispus from Wiesbaden (Germany). At the beginning of the 2nd century AD, Roman cavalrymen are shown wearing mail on the Great Trajanic Frieze

A mail shirt represented among captured Galatian weapons on a frieze from the Sanctuary of Athena Polias at Pergamon celebrating the defeat of the Tolistobogii by Attalus I, king of Pergamon (r. 241–197 BC), at some point between c.238 and 227 BC. (Photo © J.C.N. Coulston)

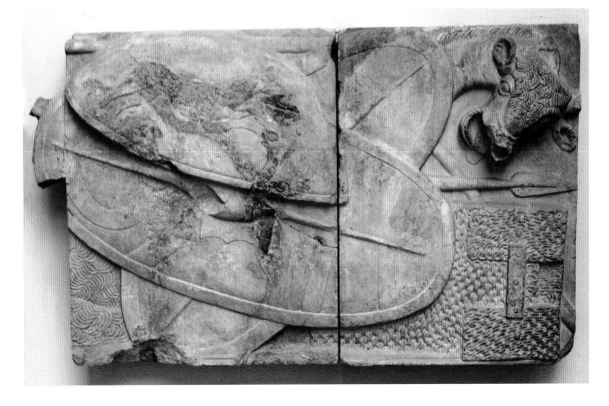

(parts of which were incorporated into the later Arch of Constantine in Rome). By contrast, on Trajan's Column, mail appears as a light, stylized pattern, now largely eroded away from the monument itself but still visible in places on the 19th-century casts of the helical frieze. By the time of the Marcus Column, 80 years later, mail armour was indicated with a series of drilled holes. The panels from a monument of Marcus Aurelius that were incorporated into the Arch of Constantine depicted mail as a highly stylized grid combining a regular pattern of incised lines and drilled holes. On the Arch of Severus in the Forum Romanum, mail was portrayed with drilled holes, sometimes within circles. For the Dominate, a relief now in the Vatican Museo Chiaramonti, possibly from the Arch of Diocletian in Rome, depicted two soldiers of the Dominate, armed with spears and the large round shields typical of the period (Bishop 2020a: 25–27), one of whom is shown wearing a long-sleeved mail cuirass, the other scale (Coulston 1990: 142).

It is likely that all Roman sculpture was painted to some degree, but Robinson's interpretation of painted mail remains controversial with those who prefer to see plain sculpted representations of body armour as depicting leather, not mail. Some idea of what painted mail on Roman tombstones may have looked like can be obtained from the stele of Salmamodes of Adada, probably a Macedonian mercenary, found in Saida (Sidon, Lebanon) and now in the İstanbul Arkeoloji Müzeleri (Turkey). The entire gravestone and its inscription have been decorated in paint with no sculpted relief component, but the mail armour is represented in various shades of grey with vertically aligned dark-grey wavy lines.

Comparison of the sculpture from Vachères, which has sculpted detailing of the mail armour, with the tombstones of Roman auxiliary cavalrymen of the 1st century AD – such as that of C. Romanius Capito from Mainz-Zahlbach (Germany) – shows many similarities. Both wear long-sleeved tunics with characteristic turned-back cuffs and the form of their armour, with shoulder guards (sometimes known as 'shoulder doubling') and breast fastening hooks, is the same. This serves to confirm that the plain sculpted depictions of the body armour of cavalrymen were indeed intended to depict mail.

Other painted representations of mail survive as murals and even manuscript illustrations. Coifs (hoods) can be seen on an illustration in the *Vergilius Vaticanus* manuscript (*Cod. Vat. Lat.* 3225) and here black dots are used to hint at mail body armour being worn with wrist-length sleeves (Coulston 1990: 145). This black-dot convention is also to be found on a Late Roman mural depicting a soldier in the Via Latina catacomb in Rome and recalls the shorthand device of indicating mail on the Marcus Column with drilled holes.

B | **REPUBLICAN ROMANS AND CELTS IN COMBAT**

Mail-clad legionary *principes* in combat with Gallic warriors of the Senones near the Adriatic coast in 283 BC. The Roman Army, under Curius Dentatus, were seeking revenge for the defeat of the army of Caecilius Metellus Denter in the battle of Arretium earlier that year (Denter himself was killed in the engagement). All of the legionaries wear thigh-length riveted mail with shoulder doubling and S-shaped breast fastening hooks while most of the Gauls wear no armour at all. Butted mail might have been worn by Gallic nobles, usually cavalrymen, perhaps as much a mark of status as it would

have been a practical form of defence, but most warriors went without. The Romans are wearing a *subarmalis* (padded garment) that is shorter than their mail lengthwise.

At this stage, in the early 3rd century BC, the Roman Army had not yet adopted the *pilum* (javelin) or *gladius* (sword), so fought with the *hasta* (thrusting spear), discarded examples of which can be seen lying around, and the *xiphos*-type short sword. They are already wearing the Montefortino form of helmet, complete with plumes, and by this time have adopted the sub-rectangular *scutum* that would go on to evolve into the classic Roman legionary shield.

©mcb

The representational evidence is particularly important when discussing the issue of the length of mail body armour. Republican depictions tend to show infantry wearing mail that reached to the mid-thigh, with those for cavalry being slightly shorter. A similar length is to be found depicted on the Adamclisi metopes at the beginning of the 2nd century AD. This is also the length of mail to be found on the Vatican Chiaramonti relief of Dominate date, so long mail defences are to be found throughout the Roman period, and the mail shirt from Vimose (Denmark), one of the few near-complete sets to survive in the archaeological record (see p. 21), also conforms to this pattern. The glaring exception is to be found, perhaps unsurprisingly, on one of the most prominent assemblages of sculptural depictions of mail: Trajan's Column. Here, Roman auxiliary infantry and cavalry wear shorter mail cuirasses, even in some cases leaving the buttocks exposed, as part of the sculptors' desire to depict the human form beneath (a Hellenizing trait). Unsurprisingly, perhaps, they were followed in this by the sculptors who produced the helical frieze of the Marcus Column. Those few auxiliary tombstones that depict mail, such as those of the infantrymen Pintaius and Firmus, or that of the auxiliary cavalryman C. Romanius Capito, which belong firmly within the tradition of extremely accurate Rhineland tombstones, would certainly seem to suggest there were shorter mail cuirasses during the early Principate, but that they fell somewhere between the extremes of Trajan's Column and the depictions of longer cuirasses. In this, they resemble the mail worn by cavalrymen on Republican reliefs, so it seems likely that there were always two lengths of mail shirt in use, neither of which resembled the depictions on the helical friezes of Trajan's Column and its Antonine imitator. By contrast, the depictions on the helmet from Tell Oum Hauran near Nawa (Syria) suggest that combining mail with *pteryges* (strips terminating in tassels, probably on a padded garment over the tunic and under the armour) allowed the use of a waist-length shirt during the Antonine period and possibly later.

History

Writing in the 1st century BC, Diodorus Siculus described the arms and armour of the Gauls, including this observation: 'Some of them have iron cuirasses of mail (ἁλυσιδωτός), but others are satisfied with the armour which Nature has given them and go into battle naked' (Diodorus Siculus, *Bibliotheca historica* 5.30.3). Strabo, writing shortly afterwards, noted of the Lusitanians in Spain that 'Most of them wear linen cuirasses; a few wear cuirasses of mail (ἁλυσιδωτός) and helmets with three crests' (Strabo, *Geography* 3.3.6).

Mail shirts shown on the Aemilius Paullus Monument at Delphi, with a cavalryman (left) and a legionary infantryman (right), identifiable by their shoulder doubling and slits at the thigh. (Photos © J.C.N. Coulston)

A statue of a mail-clad warrior (with the mail indicated by holes drilled in the surface) comes from the Gallic *oppidum* of Entremont (France), founded in the first half of the 2nd century BC and captured by the Romans in 123 BC. The aforementioned statue from Vachères, ostensibly depicting a Gallic warrior in mail, is more problematic, and may in fact represent a cavalryman in Roman service.

The bulk of excavated examples of Iron Age mail – including examples from Ciumeşti, Cetăţeni and Popeşti (all in Romania) – can be dated to the 2nd to 1st centuries BC at the earliest (Hansen 2003: 61). An example of mail from Tiefenau, a district of Bern (Switzerland), was found deposited (in water), together with Iron Age weaponry dated to the La Tène III period (2nd to 1st centuries BC). This armour was made entirely of butted rings, so it may well have been intended purely as a votive piece and never destined for serious use in battle (Müller 1986). An alternative explanation may be that the earliest forms of mail indeed employed only butted rings and the introduction of welded and riveted rings was the next stage in development.

A mail shirt from a burial at Folly Lane in St Albans (England) pre-dates the Roman invasion of Britain in AD 43 (Gilmour 1999). The method of construction, using riveted rings and solid (possibly welded) rings matches contemporary Roman finds from the Continent but is particularly noteworthy for the use of a clockwise method of winding the wire on the riveted rings (see p. 60). The possibility cannot be discounted that this is a continental import, like many other items in elite burials immediately before the Roman invasion of Britain.

The exact date of the first use of mail armour by the Romans is unknown, but it is not unreasonable to assume that, like much else, they adopted it from opponents they faced on the battlefield. They encountered various tribes that were generally identified as Gauls ('Galli') or Celts ('Celti' or 'Keltoi') from 390 BC onwards, when the Senones (a Cisalpine Gallic tribe) attacked northern Italy and, ultimately, Rome itself. They were finally defeated by the Romans in 283 BC, but this pre-dates the earliest recorded archaeological examples of mail just mentioned. This suggests that mail was not actually adopted by the Romans until well into the Punic Wars (264–146 BC), in which the Carthaginians were using Celtiberian allies against the Romans.

By the time of the depiction of the first battle of Pydna (AD 168) on the Aemilius Paullus Monument at Delphi (Greece), both Roman legionaries and what are presumably citizen cavalry were shown wearing thigh-length mail armour with shoulder guards (whereby an additional section was attached near the top of the back, incorporating shoulder pieces that were fastened to the breast). This is in fact the earliest representation of Roman mail in stone. The cavalrymen are shown with a triangular slit in both the side of the hem of the armour and the tunic beneath it, presumably to facilitate a comfortable seat upon their mount. Polybios confirms the use of mail at this time:

> The common soldiers wear in addition a breastplate of brass a span square, which they place in front of the heart and call the heart-protector (*pectorale*), this completing their accoutrements; but those who are rated above ten thousand *drachmae* wear instead of this a coat of mail (*lorica*). The *principes* and *triarii* are armed in the same manner except that, instead of *pila*, the *triarii* carry thrusting spears (*hastae*). (Polybios, *Histories* 6.23.14–16)

Mail depicted on the so-called Altar of Domitius Ahenobarbus with elliptical chisel marks on both legionary infantrymen (left) and a cavalryman (right). (Photo Jastrow/Wikimedia/ Public Domain)

Polybios uses the word ἀλυσιδωτός (*alysidotós* or 'chain-like') for mail so that there can be no doubt what is intended.

The same form of mail armour is depicted on the so-called Altar of Domitius Ahenobarbus as a series of vertically aligned, elliptical chisel marks. This monument is usually dated to the late 2nd or early 1st century BC on stylistic grounds. Indeed, this form of the mail cuirass continued in use well into the second half of the 1st century AD, with a number of examples depicted on tombstones, including that of C. Valerius Crispus from Wiesbaden, which probably dates to the early Flavian period (*c.*AD 70–85). The tombstone of C. Castricius Victor from Budapest (Hungary), which is unlikely to be much later, appears to show a one-piece mail shirt in use by the deceased, however. By the time the Adamclisi metopes were produced at the beginning of the 2nd century AD, one-piece mail cuirasses were the norm. They are also depicted on the helical frieze of Trajan's Column, although for reasons already outlined, this is perhaps less reliable than the Romanian monument.

Around the middle of the 2nd century AD, a new type of mail shirt emerged, fastened with two central, rectangular breastplates (with a cut-out for the neck of the wearer). These comparatively small pieces of plate armour featured embossed decoration and continued in use into the 3rd century AD (Bishop 2022: 32–34). When it comes to the period of the Dominate, fragments of ferrous mail from a folded cuirass were found on the site of

Detail on the cast of the pedestal of Trajan's Column in the Victoria and Albert Museum in London, illustrating how captured Dacian mail is shown in much greater detail than on the helical frieze above it, probably because it was far easier to see. (Photo © M.C. Bishop)

what is thought to have been a funeral pyre for the Emperor Galerius (r. AD 305–11), or more likely his proxy wax effigy, at the site of his palace at Gamzigrad (Serbia). The rings had been stamped with an external diameter of 13mm, internal of 6mm, and were made from ferrous sheet 2–3mm thick, giving them a rectangular cross-section. As ever, solid rings alternated with open, riveted rings (Vujović 2017).

Description

Roman mail had two principal components: a solid ring and a riveted ring (Wijnhoven 2022). These were usually made from a ferrous metal (wrought iron or steel), although occasionally a copper alloy (normally an *orichalcum* brass) was employed. Riveted rings were formed from wire, while solid rings could be formed from wire or stamped from sheet metal. Riveted rings had their overlapping terminals flattened and then pierced, once it was formed into a circle, and a rivet was then inserted through the gaps once aligned. Before the rivet was inserted, however, the rings were joined quincunx-fashion, so that each riveted ring joined four solid rings, and each welded ring was attached to four solid rings (a so-called four-in-one weave). This system saw alternating horizontal rows of solid rings and riveted rings (Wijnhoven et al. 2021: 108–09). More complex variations were introduced in the medieval period, but this simple form was the one employed throughout the Roman period.

The form of the defence constructed from this combination of rings was essentially a tube, with openings for the torso, neck and arms – much like a modern T-shirt or some forms of Roman-period tunic (Wijnhoven 2015b: 93) – as well as (sometimes) triangular gaps at the lower edge (for comfort) and, for some variants, to accommodate the insertion of fastening breastplates.

One detail that was depicted on Trajan's Column (and mimicked on other representational media, such as the Marcus Column and a small, unprovenanced, copper-alloy figurine now in the British Museum in London), namely a serrated (or 'dagged') lower hem, has never been found on any archaeological examples, nor is it shown on earlier figured tombstones. This detail may have come about through confusion on the part of the sculptors

A section of (slightly rusty) reconstructed, four-in-one stamped and riveted mail demonstrating two different orientations of a 'weave', with riveted rings oriented horizontally (left) and vertically (right). (Photo © M.C. Bishop)

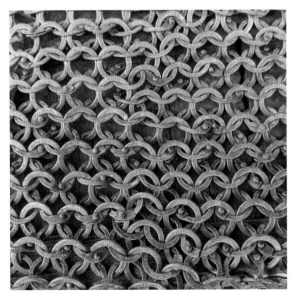
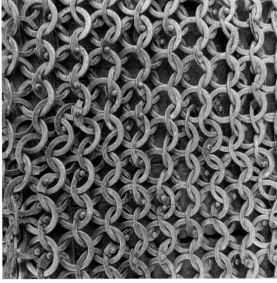

of the helical frieze of Trajan's Column over a fringed, padded garment worn under the armour (see p. 57), which was then copied by metropolitan artists.

Groller found examples of mail in the *Waffenmagazin* at Carnuntum (1901b: 114) near Bad Deutsch-Altenburg (Austria), but was confused by some of the more heavily corroded chunks into believing that there was a form of armour woven from wire (rather than in discrete rings), which he described as *Drahtpanzer* ('wire armour') or *lorica reticulata*, as he termed it.

Variants

The earliest form of Roman mail attested by representational evidence is the two-piece mail defence, in which a simple tube of joined rings had an extension – or, alternatively, an additional section attached (Wijnhoven 2022: Fig. 10.25) – to the top of the back which, divided into two broad sections, was brought over the shoulders and fastened at the chest (as shoulder guards). In this, it may have imitated the form of the Greek linen cuirass (*ibid*.: 247–49). This is the form of mail armour depicted on the Aemilius Paullus Monument and the 'Gallic warrior' from Vachères, and it can be seen being worn by the cavalryman Flavius Bassus on his tombstone from Cologne (Germany). The fasteners for this form of mail armour are depicted on the frieze on the temple of Athena Polias at Pergamon, the Vachères warrior, on a relief of Mars from Mavilly-Mandelot (France), as well as on the tombstone relief of the auxiliary cavalryman C. Romanius Capito and the auxiliary infantry standard-bearer (*signifer*) Sex. Valerius Genialis from Mainz (Germany). Actual examples have been recovered from a number of excavations, including Longthorpe (England) and the tomb of a cavalryman at Chassenard (France), where one fastener was still attached to a mail shirt stored inside the face-mask of a cavalry 'sports' helmet. The Roman versions of such fasteners were attached to the centre of the upper chest with a large rivet, around which they could pivot, allowing their recurved terminals to hook over studs on the shoulder pieces and secure them in place. Both the legionaries and Roman cavalrymen on the Aemilius Paullus Monument wear armour that covers the buttocks and groin (often referred to, rather imprecisely, as 'thigh-length') and the same is true of auxiliary troops like C. Romanius Capito in the early Principate.

Ultimately, a one-piece form of cuirass began to be adopted in the latter part of the 1st century AD, to the extent that Trajan's Column and the Tropaeum Traiani monument at Adamclisi give the impression that it had been universally accepted by the early 2nd century AD. Whether this was indeed the case is difficult to judge on the limited available evidence, although most examples of mail fasteners from stratified deposits belong within the 1st century AD. This seems to have mimicked the design of the tunic (Wijnhoven 2022: 239–42).

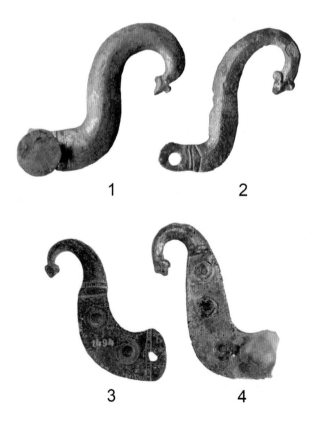

Mail fastening hooks of copper alloy from the legionary fortresses of Carnuntum (**1–2**) and of Vindonissa at Windisch (**3–4**). In each case, only half of the fastening survives and both 1 and 4 retain the central hinge rivet. (Photos © Andreas Pangerl)

1   2

3   4

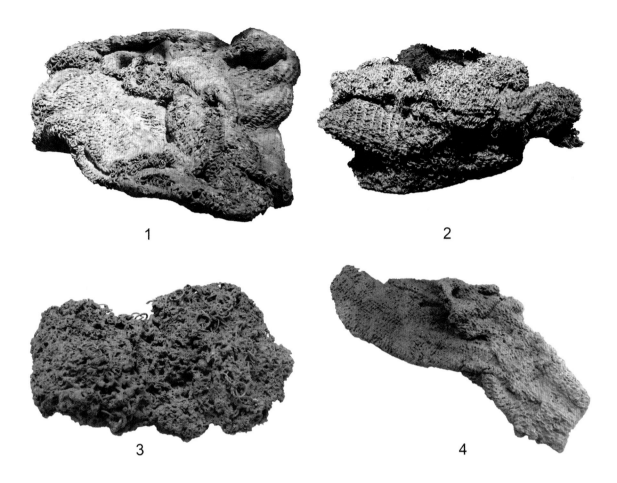

1   2

3   4

Complete or near-complete mail shirts from Roman fortifications on the Upper German/Raetian and Danubian *limites*: Zugmantel (**1**), Aalen (**2**), Enns (**3**) and Weißenburg (**4**). (Photos © M.C. Bishop (1), Wolfgang Sauber/Wikimedia/CC-BY-SA 4.0 (2), Wolfgang Sauber/Wikimedia/CC-BY-SA 3.0 (3–4))

The middle of the 2nd century AD saw the introduction of breastplated mail defences (at the same time as the introduction of this type of fastening for scale shirts; see p. 34). This form of body armour had an enlarged opening at the neck that was then secured by means of two opposing sheet-metal plates with embossed decoration (which also helped to strengthen them through corrugation), fastened with a pair of turning pins (Bishop 2022: 32–34). A variant of this form found at Bertoldsheim (Germany) incorporated a narrower two-piece fastening and this may represent a corresponding backplate opening (D'Amato & Negin 2017: 91–104); other examples of such plates are known from Budapest (Hungary), Enns (Austria) and Ritopek (Serbia). The plates were attached to an aperture in the cuirass by means of disc-headed rivets (decorated with moulded, concentric rings) on the long, outer edge, but not normally on the shorter, lower edge. The number of rivets varied between four and six (although this was sometimes increased by additional holes having been punched as a result of repairs) and seems to have been a matter of preference on the part of the armourer. This form of mail armour does not seem to have lasted beyond the middle of the 3rd century AD, however.

Whether the one-piece mail cuirass ever completely disappeared is doubtful, but it certainly returned to popularity during the 3rd century AD and remained the principal form of this type of defence (so far as it is possible to tell) throughout the Dominate. It is this form of mail that was found at Zugmantel (Greiner 2008: 97) and Rainau-Buch (*ibid*.: 97–101) on the

The South Shields mail

In 1997, excavation of a 3rd-century AD barrack block within the Roman fort at South Shields (England) revealed the remains of a complete mail shirt (Croom 2001). This was buried when a conflagration towards the end of the 3rd or beginning of the 4th century AD caused the building to collapse, the mail shirt being found on the floor in a suite of rooms at the east end, interpreted as part of the officers' quarters. Protected by building material from the worst of the fire (there was daub both under and over it, suggesting it was not actually lying on the floor before the collapse), the mail shirt survived in good condition, although the rings were almost completely oxidized.

The solid rings employed for this cuirass had an external diameter of 7mm, while the riveted rings were mostly larger, at around 8mm, and tended towards oval in shape. The rivets were around 1mm in diameter, inserted through flattened terminals c.1.75mm in width. Some of the rings were observed to have lost their rivets. All of the rings were made of circular-sectioned wire with a diameter that ranged between 1.0 and 1.8mm. It has been suggested that the solid rings were perhaps welded, and there were no clear indications of butt joins or stamping.

No obvious openings could be detected and X-raying the armour revealed that there were no fastening plates or other attachments.

German *limes* (pl. *limites*; frontier fortifications), and South Shields in England (Croom 2001). It has already been noted that an illustration in the *Vergilius Vaticanus* manuscript seems to indicate that coifs could sometimes be incorporated in defences, presumably in place of helmets.

Two examples of non-Roman mail cuirasses are worth consideration here for their intimate relationship with (and possibly influence by) the Roman world. Excavation of the Sassanid Persian siege mine under Tower 19 at Dura-Europos (Syria) led to the discovery of what were evidently the remains of one of the attackers, still clad in a mail shirt. It had baggy, three-quarter-length sleeves and appears originally to have reached to the thigh, although for various reasons it had been pulled up at or soon after the time of the attacker's death. The lower hem was edged with copper-alloy rings and a trident-shaped device was incorporated into the weave of the armour centrally, below the neck opening, also using copper-alloy rings. Corrosion products on the inside of the mail may have preserved fibres from a long, felt, padded undergarment (James 2004: 116).

An unusually well-preserved, one-piece mail shirt composed of stamped and riveted ferrous rings was recovered from what was originally a watery

A ferrous mail shirt found in the ruins of a burnt-down 3rd-century AD barrack building in the fort at South Shields. (Photo © Arbeia Roman Fort)

context as a 'bog' find at Vimose. The neck opening is configured as a simple slit in the fabric that could be closed by means of strap fittings to narrow the gap and prevent the armour slipping off one or the other shoulder. Short-sleeved and reaching to the knee, the armour appears to have been deliberately damaged, much as described by Paulus Orosius (*Historiae Adversum Paganos* 5.16.5–6) in his account of the aftermath of the Roman defeat at the battle of Arausio (105 BC). This may have been achieved by tearing the cuirass upwards from the slits that it would have needed at either side of the hem to facilitate walking. A number of factors, including riveted ring shape and ring size, have led to it being argued that the Vimose defence was locally manufactured, although it is clearly heavily influenced by Roman mail (Wijnhoven 2015b).

Finally, one other type of very fine mail cuirass, which combines the use of scales (and is often termed '*lorica plumata*'), is considered below (see p. 34).

Once conserved, the mail shirt was found to weigh 5.44kg, although the fact that the rings were almost completely oxidized meant that it will have lost some mass. For comparison, a modern replica mail shirt with similar-sized butted, and not riveted, rings weighs 6.6kg (rivets would make it even heavier), but note the comments below on mail density (see p. 46).

Dimensions of some examples of pre-Roman and Roman mail armour*						
Cuirass	Period	Ring exterior diameter	Ring interior diameter	Ring thickness	Mail type	Material
Ciumești	Iron Age	8.9/8.0mm	5.5/5.5mm	1.6/1.3mm	regular	fe
Tiefenau	Iron Age	13.0mm	10.0mm	1.0mm	regular	fe
Augsburg	Roman (1st)	3.8–4.2mm	2.8mm	0.5–0.7mm	hybrid	ae
Bizye (Vize)	Roman (1st)	3.0–4.0mm	?	?	hybrid	ae
Chassenard	Roman (1st)	c.4.5mm	?	?	regular	fe
Ouddorp	Roman (1st)	3.2/4.3mm	2.2/2.9mm	0.2mm	hybrid	ae
The Lunt	Roman (1st)	3.0mm	1.7/2.0mm	0.5/1.0mm	hybrid?	ae
Usk 7	Roman (1st)	3.0mm	c.1.0mm	c.1.0mm	hybrid	fe
Carlingwark Loch	Roman (1st/2nd)	7.3/7.0mm	5.0/5.0mm	1.1/1.0mm	regular	fe
Newstead 4	Roman (2nd)	4.1mm	2.8mm	0.7/0.3mm	hybrid	ae
Zemplin	Roman (2nd)	8.0/9.0mm	6.2/7.0mm	1.4mm	regular	fe
Dura-Europos 1	Sassanid (3rd)	c.8.0mm	c.6.0mm	1.0mm	decorated	fe/ae
Bertoldsheim	Roman (3rd)	7.7/7.0mm	5.5/5.1mm	0.7–0.9mm	decorated	fe/ae
Künzing 3	Roman (3rd)	7.6/7.6mm	5.2/4.44mm	1.0–1.3/1.1–1.4mm	regular	fe
Rainau-Buch 2	Roman (3rd)	10.0/7.5mm	?	?	regular	fe
South Shields 1	Roman (3rd)	7.0/8.0mm	6.0/7.0mm	3.33–7.0mm	regular	fe
Zugmantel	Roman (3rd)	8.0/10.0mm	?	?	regular	fe
Gamzigrad	Roman (3rd/4th)	13.0mm	6.0mm	3.0mm	regular	fe
Stari Jankovci	Roman (3rd/4th)	14.0mm	8.4mm	3.0/2.6mm	regular	fe

* For cuirass numbering see Wijnhoven 2022.

Details on the cast of the pedestal of Trajan's Column in the Victoria and Albert Museum showing captured scale armour. (Photos © M.C. Bishop)

Fresco depicting infantrymen wearing (silvered?) scale armour with coifs on the battle of Eben-Ezer panel from the synagogue at Dura-Europos. Two cavalrymen wear undetailed grey garments that may be intended to represent mail or, possibly, just tunics. (Yale University Art Gallery Dura-Europos Collection/ Public Domain)

SCALE ARMOUR

Scale armour relied for its defensive strength on overlapping its individual component scales (*squamae*) downwards, mimicking the natural overlap (from head to tail) of fish scales. Each scale was partially covered by the scale above it and in turn partly covered the one below it. Similarly, each scale was overlapped by its neighbour to one side as well as overlapping its neighbour on the other side. This was arranged in such a way that the twists of wire or stitching that joined neighbouring scales were always concealed by an overlying neighbour.

Sculpture is no less important for understanding the use of scale by the Roman Army than it is for mail. It is also much easier to be certain when it was depicted, since no artistic shortcuts (such as using paint to indicate mail) seem to have been used. Scale is found on provincial military tombstones

of both legionary and auxiliary troops in the 1st century AD and also occurs on the Adamclisi metopes and on the Great Trajanic Frieze. Trajan's Column, however, reserves scale for the display of captured weaponry and equipment that adorns the pedestal, as well as for specialist troops on the helical frieze, notably Roman auxiliary archers. Although usually identified as 'Eastern' archers, these men have helmets and tunics similar to those of the northern Danubian tribes like the Iazyges and Rhoxolāni, and non-metallic scale was also a common form of armour among steppe peoples. The Marcus Column was less dogmatic in its armour differentiation than its Trajanic predecessor and Roman troops are there shown wearing segmental, mail and scale armour (usually arranged in repeating patterns). This was also true of the panels from a monument of Marcus Aurelius on the Arch of Constantine, on which scale body armour is depicted.

Tombstone of the cavalryman Vonatorix, shown wearing scale body armour with shoulder doubling and *pteryges* at the sleeves. (Photo © M.C. Bishop)

The 1st-century AD tombstone evidence shows scale armour mostly being used by auxiliary cavalryman, such as Vonatorix from Bonn (Germany) and Longinus from Colchester, and junior legionary officers, like the two Sertorius brothers from Verona (Italy) – an *aquilifer* (eagle-bearer) and a centurion, both serving in *legio XI Claudia*.

Sculptural representations of scale armour often incorporate a central longitudinal ridge for each scale, although this is not a common feature of excavated scales except with hybrid mail and scale cuirasses (see p. 34).

The wall paintings from the synagogue at Dura-Europos depict figures of biblical tales in what was then contemporary costume, and some of these included soldiers. Infantrymen in the battle of Eben-Ezer fresco panel wear what is probably intended to be scale armour, possibly tinned or silvered, and they (like the mail-clad soldiers of the *Vergilius Vaticanus* manuscript illustration; see p. 12) are depicted wearing coifs, rather than helmets, to protect their heads, necks and throats.

As with mail armour, evidently the length of scale cuirasses could vary. Although the sculptors of the helical frieze of Trajan's Column chose not to associate them with Roman regular troops, the men carving the Marcus Column depicted scale cuirasses as waist length, similar to mail shirts. The Adamclisi metopes, on the other hand, have scale of the same length as the mail, so reaching to the lower thighs. This length is also shown on the scale-clad Dominate soldier on the Vatican Chiaramonti relief. The Sertorius brothers wear shorter scale armour, while the cavalryman Vonatorix wears a scale cuirass with a side split that reaches to the upper thigh. Again, the impression is given that there were different lengths of scale armour throughout the Roman period and that this was a direct result of the troop type for which any given cuirass was intended. Some of the shorter cuirasses – such as those of the Sertorius brothers – were terminated in a double row of semicircular lappets, possibly in imitation of muscled cuirasses like that shown on the Antonine funerary *tondo* from Seggauberg in Austria (Bishop 2022: 42).

History

Scale armour is first recorded from Bronze Age Egypt (Dawson 2013: 26), but a set of Roman scale armour in the Royal Ontario Museum in Toronto, Canada, purchased from an art dealer in the 1930s and alleged to have been found near the site of the battle of Lake Trasimene (217 BC), is now largely accepted to be a modern concoction using a variety of disparate ancient components (Robinson 1975: 154, Pls 434–35). Development of scale armour in the Near and Middle East continued into the Iron Age and Roman periods, as is shown by finds of this type of armour from Masada (Israel), apparently belonging to the Jewish defenders, rather than the Roman attackers, in the 1st century AD. Such scales are markedly different from those in Roman use, with a characteristic broad central ridge and raised periphery, and with only sufficient holes to attach the scales to a fabric backing and not their horizontal (or vertical) neighbours.

Roman troops were not depicted wearing scale armour until the beginning of the Principate. No scales are known from the Augustan occupation of Germania east of the Rhine, and it was probably first adopted by the Roman Army in the western provinces at the very end of the emperor Augustus' rule (r. 27 BC–AD 14), or during the Tiberio-Claudian period, perhaps as a result of increased contact with eastern troops.

Tacitus provided an interesting description of a Roman encounter with armoured Sarmatian cavalry:

No troops could show so little spirit when fighting on foot; when they charge in squadrons, hardly any line can stand against them. But as on this occasion the day was damp and the ice thawed, what with the continual slipping of their horses, and the weight of their armour, they could make no use of their lances or their swords, which being of an excessive length they wield with both hands. These defences, worn by the princes and most distinguished persons of the tribe, are formed of plates of iron or very tough hide, and although they are absolutely impenetrable to blows, yet they make it difficult for those

Scales found at Masada and thought to have belonged to the defenders during the Roman siege of AD 73–74. (Superikonoskop/Wikimedia/ CC-BY-SA 3.0)

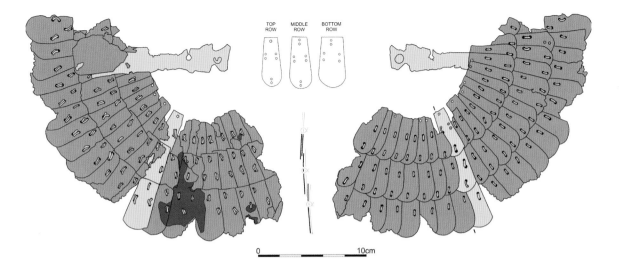

TOP ROW | MIDDLE ROW | BOTTOM ROW

0   10cm

brought down by an enemy charge to get back up again. Besides, the Sarmatians were perpetually sinking in the deep and soft snow. The Roman soldier, attacking easily in his cuirass, continued to harass them with javelins and lances, and whenever the occasion required, closed with them with his short sword, and stabbed the defenceless Sarmatians; for it is not their custom to defend themselves with a shield. (Tacitus, *Hist.* 1.79)

Cavalry matching that description are shown on Trajan's Column, with both riders and horses clad in scale armour. Scale is depicted in use by legionaries on the Adamclisi metopes, and it is also shown on the Marcus Column being used by both Roman auxiliary infantry and cavalry.

Scale armour continued in use during the 3rd century AD, as attested by finds from abandonment deposits at Dura-Europos and the German *limes*. Moreover, iconographic evidence indicates that it continued in currency into the Dominate, although its comparative rarity from archaeological sites of this later period does not serve to confirm this.

Part of the upper section around the collar of a set of ferrous semi-rigid scale armour from Carlisle. It employs three different types of scale for its three rows, the top one of which has holes for the attachment of leather binding. Each of the other scales is wired to its neighbour to either side and above and below (except for the bottom row). One column of scales is of brass, as is the wire used throughout. (Drawing © M.C. Bishop)

Description

In its most basic form, scale body armour consisted of rows of individual scales, with sets of peripheral holes (among the Carnuntum material, Groller noted a minimum of four and a maximum of 12). Roman scales were joined to their neighbours on either side with a twist of wire, using the holes at the side, each row then being sewn to a flexible backing, by means of the hole or holes near the top. Roman scale armour appears to have been the first to have used wire to connect adjoining plates. The backing was usually textile of some kind, although examples have been found in which leather has been used. As well as providing a means of articulation for a cuirass, the backing also served to protect underlying garments from damage caused by the edges and corners of the scales or the ends of the wire twists (which were usually folded over at the rear, not at the front face, of the armour). The scales in each row thus had a limited amount of movement horizontally, but much more vertically, due to the underlying backing garment. That said, there was an inevitable compromise in the defensive qualities of the armour, since there was an obvious vulnerability to an upwards thrust of a blade.

The tombstones from Verona of the two Sertorius brothers, serving in *legio XI Claudia*, based at Windisch. One (Q. Sertorius Festus) was a centurion, the other (L. Sertorius Firmus) an *aquilifer*, and both were depicted wearing scale armour. (Photos © M.C. Bishop)

Organic components only rarely survive, principally as organics in anaerobic conditions, as happened to the leather and textile of the Carpow (Scotland) armour; or as mineralized 'fossils', where their cell structure has been replaced by minerals leeching out of corrosion products from the armour to which they were attached (as in the Carnuntum *Waffenmagazin*; see p. 52). By observing the mineralized remains of threads, Groller identified five variations on the method of attaching scales to their underlying garment, depending upon whether they had one, two or four holes at the top of the scale.

The first variant, for scales with just two holes aligned parallel to the top edge of the scale (Groller's type V), saw a single strand that passed up through one hole and down through its neighbour. The second variant, for scales with two holes perpendicular to the top edge of the scale (types IV, VI and VII), saw a pair of strands, alternately passing above and below the scales of a row. The third variant was found on scales with four holes (types I and VIII) and simply doubled the number of strands to that of the first variant. A fourth variant was used with single-holed scales (type III) whereby a single strand passed over the top of the scale then down through the hole and so to the neighbouring scale. A fifth variant simply saw a short strand passed through two larger vertical holes (type IX) and knotted on the underside. Groller offered no explanation as to how his type II scales (one large hole in each upper corner) were attached to the underlying garment.

The underlying garments were mostly made out of twisted two- or three-strand linen yarn (flax) but some leather was used too, chiefly with single-holed (Groller's type III) scales. Study of the Carnuntum finds also revealed that, where mineralized fragments were found adhering to sets of scales, there was straw present. As at Carpow, linen was used for the underlying garment, as well as leather, and straw was employed to pad it.

©mcb

0   20cm

Each row of scales was in part overlapped by the row above and, in turn, partly covered the row below. This meant that the wire ties securing the scales horizontally and the stitching attaching the row to the underlying garment were concealed and were always covered by the lowest part of the scales of the row above. Scales were also depicted on monuments, arranged so that they were offset by half the width of the scale in the row below.

The development of semi-rigid scale was perhaps a response to this vulnerability. Each scale was not only attached to its neighbours horizontally, but also vertically, with wire twists. The drawback with this system is that storage then became an issue, since such a cuirass could not be collapsed or folded (as with the Carpow armour) without dismantling it into halves in much the same way as a muscled cuirass of plate armour. Unlike standard scale armour, the semi-rigid form overlapped in a different way from top to bottom, since the wiring holes at the bottom of each scale had to align with those in the centre of the top of the next scale down, which meant that no offset was possible. In this way, the standard and semi-rigid forms were visually, as well as functionally, very different.

Examples of scale armour found during excavations in the fort at Carlisle (England) demonstrate how individual scales would be tapered inwards from

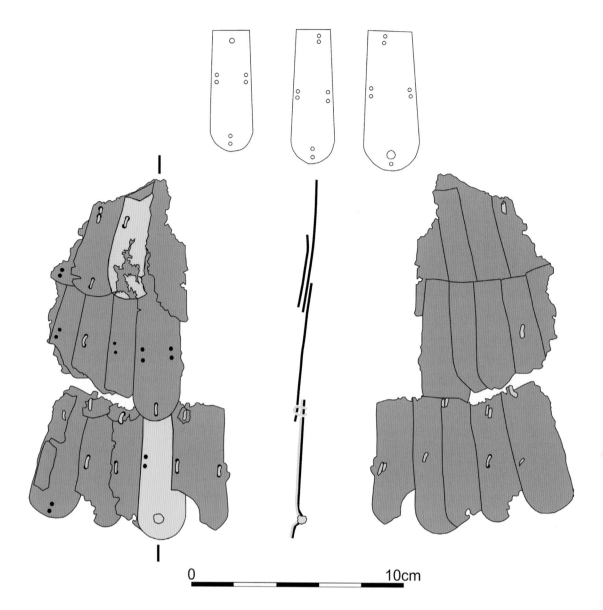

0   10cm

A portion of ferrous semi-rigid scale from Carlisle. Alternate scales have separate, overlying brass plates for decorative effect. (Drawing © M.C. Bishop)

bottom to top in order to shape the top of the cuirass around the neck. The Carpow cuirass retained fragmentary leather edging strips, confirming a detail depicted on some iconography. These would then have been employed around the lower hem, as well as the neck and arm openings, along with any junction down the side (or sides) of a cuirass, which would have been necessary to facilitate putting a cuirass on or taking it off.

SEMI-RIGID SCALE ARMOUR IN THE MARCOMANNIC WARS

A *centuria* of legionaries of *legio II Adiutrix* on patrol in the valley of the Granus (Hron) River, a tributary to the north of the Danube River in Marcomannia. Most are wearing semi-rigid scale with embossed breast fastening plates, but there are also some similarly equipped mail shirts as well as a few examples of the Newstead type of *lorica*

segmentata. By now, all of the men wear the *subarmalis* with *pteryges*.

The main column of legionaries, marching on an unsurfaced track with tree stumps betraying the fact that it has recently been cleared for a bowshot on either side, are accompanied by a screen of light auxiliary infantry (wearing mail) on the flanks and to the front and rear, while auxiliary cavalry (in scale and mail) can be seen even further out.

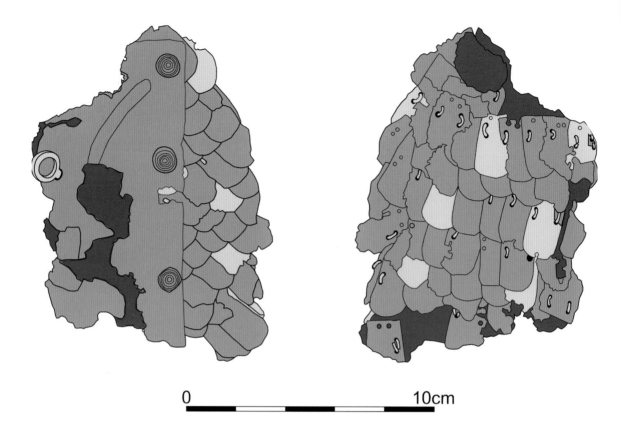

0   10cm

A portion of flexible scale armour from Carlisle. It includes part of a ferrous breastplate and most of the scales are likewise ferrous, but every fourth scale in each row is of copper alloy, again for decorative effect. (Drawing © M.C. Bishop)

Variants

Fabric-backed scale armour was the norm during the 1st and early 2nd centuries AD and continued in use later. The evidence from Carnuntum suggests that the foundation garment, whether of linen or leather, may have included padding in the form of straw, although it is entirely possible that this was a detail peculiar to that particular site. It does, however, have some relevance to any discussion of the use of a padded garment worn under mail or scale armour (see p. 57).

More than 300 copper-alloy scales are known from Ham Hill in Somerset (England) and probably date to soon after the period of the Roman invasion of Britain, when a number of Iron Age hillforts were occupied by Roman forces. Alternately tinned, the scales belonged to Groller's type V, with pairs of holes to either side for attachment to their neighbours and a pair at the top for sewing to the foundation garment.

Some copper-alloy scales from Corbridge (England), although also of Groller's type V, differed in being smaller than the Ham Hill assemblage and having a pointed rather than rounded base, arguably easier and quicker to produce (Anstee 1953).

A collection of 1mm-thick brass scales was recovered from one of the rooms in the headquarters building at Newstead (England), so datable to its Antonine abandonment around AD 180 – and these were of Groller's type III, with pairs of holes for wire twists to either side and a single, central hole at the top for attachment to the undergarment (Curle 1911: 158–59 & Pl. XXIV).

The development of semi-rigid scale armour in the first half of the 2nd century AD solved some of the problems associated with regular scale cuirasses but in turn created its own, new ones. A reduction in flexibility must have been one of the major drawbacks, because now any 'give' in the defence was entirely dependent upon the amount of play in the wire twists joining each scale to its neighbours.

A curving section of semi-flexible scale armour from around the neck opening (overlapping left over right and probably from the shoulder) was excavated from an early 2nd century AD context at Carlisle (Bishop 2009: 689) and conveniently illustrates how one cuirass would actually be built up from a variety of different types of scale. All of the 21 scales recovered (still articulated) were tapered so that they were narrower at the top than at the bottom, thereby facilitating the overall curved shape of the fragment. The top row of scales had a single, central hole in the upper edge (probably to attach a leather binding, which was missing), along with pairs of holes at either side and at the bottom (a variant of Groller's type VII). The second (middle) row had pairs of holes at the top and bottom and to either side (Groller's type VII). Finally, the bottom row had pairs of holes to either side and at the top (Groller's type V). The scales in each row were all of similar height, but increased in width towards the bottom. All of them were ferrous except for a single scale in each row, arranged one above the other, and these were made of brass, a decorative feature that may have marked the centre line of the shoulder on one side of the defence. The ferrous scales were 1mm thick, while those of copper alloy were 0.5mm and a modern reconstruction of the excavated section, using similar materials, weighed 1.01kg (David Sim, pers. comm.).

A small patch of semi-flexible ferrous scales (overlapping right over left) from the same site incorporated a rather unusual, presumably decorative

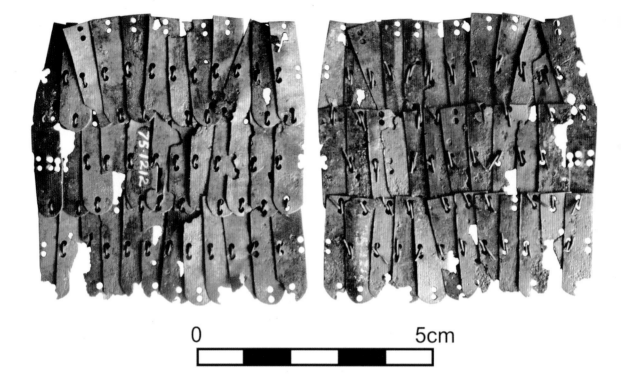

0   5cm

A section of semi-rigid scale armour from Corbridge, showing the outer (left) and inner (right) surfaces. Found in the ditches of the fort that lay beneath the later town, the anaerobic conditions prevented corrosion forming. A single scale of this type from the site led Robinson to believe (mistakenly) that it belonged to lamellar armour. (Photo © M.C. Bishop)

detail. Here, some of the ferrous scales had additional copper-alloy examples attached to the front of them using the normal wire twists. These scales also tapered upwards and the top row again had just single holes (for binding), indicating that this was again a neck opening section.

One variation on the semi-rigid scales from Carlisle seems to have appeared fairly soon afterwards as the smaller, copper-alloy scale from numerous sites such as Corbridge, Mušov (Czech Republic) and Cífer (Slovakia). As well as being smaller, these were much narrower in proportion to their height than the earlier scales from Carlisle. This begs the question as to why this change in individual scale size occurred. Part of the answer undoubtedly lay in the familiar compromise between weight and protection. The Cífer scales would yield a weight of around 2.37kg/m^2 (Cheben & Ruttkay 2010: 313, Abb.5) but it is possible that the smaller scales could have been produced by stamping, thus speeding up the manufacturing process from sheet brass.

D   **GLADIATORS USING MAIL AND SCALE ARM DEFENCES**

Two gladiators are in training in the Ludus Magnus gladiatorial school in Rome. One, a *retiarius* ('net man'; **1**) equipped with the familiar net and trident, wears a ferrous mail *manica* on his left hand, along with a shoulder guard which replaces the shield he cannot use because of the need to handle the trident with both hands. He is matched against a traditional opponent, the *murmillo* ('little fish'; **2**), who is wearing a decorated helmet, padding around both lower legs, carrying a curved, rectangular shield similar to that used by legionaries, and has a ferrous scale *manica* on his arm above his right hand, in which he holds the standard gladiator's short sword (*gladius*).

The whole scene is being watched by some members of the emperor's mounted bodyguard (**3**, **4**, **5**), the *equites singularis Augusti*, who are clearly showing an interest in the form of the combatants, with a view to backing a favourite in the forthcoming games. The soldiers are clad in scale body armour with fairly small *squamae*. The bout is also being watched by another gladiator (**6**), this time a *Thraex* (a prisoner of war captured from the Thracians), who has taken his helmet off and put his shield down, but is still wearing an articulated plate *manica* of brass on his sword arm, his curved *sica* hanging from a cord attached to his wrist and to the pommel of the sword.

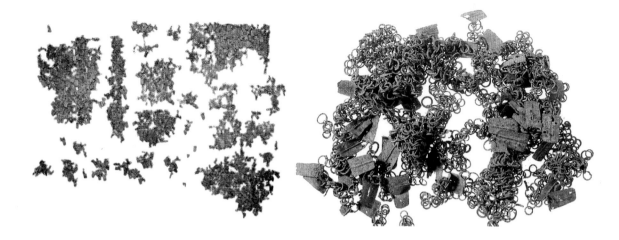

Hybrid mail and scale armour of copper alloy from Ouddorp. (Photos Rijksmuseum van Oudheden, Leiden)

The reduced flexibility of semi-rigid scale may have been one of the reasons for the introduction of breastplated cuirasses. Here, as with mail armour, pairs of decorated plates were inserted below the neck opening and attached with disc-headed rivets. When unfastened, such plates made it easier for the wearer to don the cuirass and they could then be secured by means of a pair of turning pins, examples of which have been found *in situ*.

Not all breastplated scale cuirasses were semi-rigid. Part of a breastplate and its attached scales (overlapping left over right) were found in the same deposit as the neck section just mentioned (Bishop 2009: 691). The scales were mostly ferrous, but on every other row, one in four scales was made of copper alloy, which would have produced a rather unusual pattern in the complete cuirass. The type V scales were 25mm high and 15mm wide. The ferrous breastplate (in and of itself unusual, since these items were usually of copper alloy) was embossed and retained one of the turning pins used as a fastening. The plate, which was riveted to the scales with circular, disc-headed rivets decorated with concentric moulding, is one of the earliest attested examples of this type of fastening.

One of the more unusual variants of scale armour in the 1st and 2nd centuries AD was a hybrid form that saw small scales attached to the exterior of fine mail armour in what has often been identified with a literary reference to *lorica plumata*. There are difficulties with this identification, however, and it has been proposed (Wijnhoven 2009a) that this hybrid form of armour should be referred to as '*lorica hamata squamataque*' (a modern-day term, literally meaning 'mail and scale armour'). A number of

Hybrid mail and scale armour from Rome and subsequently bought by the Altes Museum in Berlin. The whereabouts of this fragment are unknown. After Rose 1904–06, Figs 14a and 14b. (Author's collection)

examples of this type of armour are now known, including provenanced examples from Augsburg (Germany), Newstead, Usk (Wales) and Bizye (modern-day Vize in Turkey), as well as some unprovenanced examples, such as one fragment (now lost) said to come from Rome, among which the most complete is that from Ouddorp in the Netherlands (Wijnhoven 2009b). Sections of fine, copper-alloy mail found in the forts at The Lunt at Baginton (England) and under the later town at Xanten (Germany) were probably more examples of this type of armour, having lost their scales before deposition for reasons unknown.

Since this type of cuirass was essentially embellished mail, the limited evidence available (principally the defences from Bizye and Augsburg) suggests that some at least were secured by means of pairs of fastening hooks like those used on regular mail with shoulder reinforces. The Bizye armour uniquely preserved part of its linen undergarment, stitched directly to the mail around the shoulders but unattached at the lower edge; this material was beige in colour and incorporated a purple stripe (*ibid.*, 15). Since the stripe would not have been visible, it is possible the lining was a replacement employing a repurposed tunic.

Another hybrid form of armour, depicted on a relief from Alba Iulia (Romania), appears to marry segmental girth hoops on the abdominal area with breastplated scale for the upper body and shoulders (Bishop 2022: 31). Archaeologically, the components of such a cuirass could be very difficult to identify as anything other than ordinary scale or segmental armour unless a complete cuirass was found more or less intact.

Scale armour could even be found on soldiers' headgear in the form of an aventail or flexible neck guard and examples are depicted on the pedestal reliefs at the base of Trajan's Column, on helmets possibly exhibiting Sarmatian influence. A copper-alloy, conical Roman helmet from Bryastovets (Bulgaria) possessed a series of holes around the occipital region of the bowl

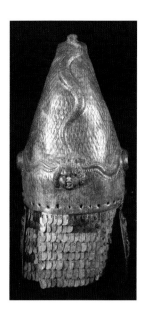

Unprovenanced copper-alloy pseudo-Attic helmet with a scale aventail. (Photo © MACM (Musée d'Art Classique de Mougins) 2022)

A remarkably intact copper-alloy scale horse trapper from Dura-Europos, with both the fabric backing and leather edging surviving. (Photos Yale University Art Gallery)

Fragments of another scale horse armour from Dura-Europos that demonstrates something of the structure of the trapper. Scales can be seen wired horizontally to their neighbours through the pairs of holes on either side and sewn to the backing fabric through the four holes at the top of each scale. (Photo Yale University Art Gallery)

in place of a standard neck guard intended to attach just such a scale aventail (D'Amato & Negin 2017: Fig. 80a–b). Another, more complete example, this time a pseudo-Attic helmet, unprovenanced and now in the Musée d'Art Classique de Mougins (France), retained its aventail of small copper-alloy scales.

The excavations at Dura-Europos produced two near-complete sets (and several fragments) of horse armour formed from scales attached to a textile backing. This backing was made up of two layers of fabric, the inner of which was finer than the outer, and with the scales sewn through both layers. Worn over the horse harness, and with an opening for the saddle, the scales of the trappers (one with copper-alloy scales, now in the National Museum of Damascus, and one with ferrous scales, now in Yale University) were arranged to descend from the line of the spine of the horse. Beyond the normal holes for wiring scales to their neighbours horizontally and those employed for stitching the rows to the fabric backing, additional holes were added to attach strips of leather edging (dyed red) to the defence. Some of the

E   **SCALE-CLAD HORSES AT DURA-EUROPOS**

Hot and dusty armoured Roman horsemen from the part-mounted *cohors XX Palmyrenorum* return to the military compound in Dura-Europos during the early 3rd century AD after a patrol. One horse in the foreground is equipped with an iron scale trapper and a mail crinet (armour for the neck of the horse). The horse's head is protected by a rather battered

copper-alloy chamfron with integral eyeguards and still retaining some traces of tinning from its glory days being used in cavalry training and display exercises known as the *hippika gymnasia*. The second horse has a copper-alloy trapper, along with a crinet, made of the same material. The chamfron, however, is leather covered with disc studs overlapped to resemble scales.

scales pierced in this way appear to have been used to repair the armour in a number of places, since redundant edging holes can be found in the middle of the sets of scales. Other repairs are betrayed by changes to the way in which scales overlap (James 2004: 129–34).

The sets of horse armour found in the collapsed Tower 19 hint that the unit of Palmyrenes, although only a part-mounted cohort, were nevertheless using at least some horse armour. The realities of frontier life seldom matched the theoretical norms. There are also three possible scale cuisses (thigh guards) from Dura-Europos, two of copper alloy and one of iron (*ibid.*: 125–26). The copper-alloy pieces come from Tower 19 and one of them retains its fabric backing. The scales themselves were sewn to the backing by a 'double helix' system of stitching that ensures that even if one thread broke a scale would still be held secure. The scales of the iron fragment were larger and match the ferrous horse trapper (see table below), although the overall shape of the defence matches other cuisses from the site.

An unusual variant of scale armour was excavated from Caerleon (Wales), apparently adorning a leather chamfron from horse armour. Here, circular copper-alloy studs were overlapped in such a way that they resembled *squamae* of more traditional scale armour (Anon 2014).

One item of mail or scale armour that is familiar from a civilian context – the armguard (*manica*) worn by gladiators – is not so far attested in the military sphere, in complete contrast to armguards made of articulated plate armour (Bishop 2022: 34–39). A *venator* ('hunter') gladiator on a fresco from the amphitheatre at Mérida (Spain) was depicted wearing what seems to be mail covering his entire left arm, while gladiators on the Villa Borghese mosaic from Rome are unambiguously shown with scale *manicae*. The reason for the adoption of the plate version by the military, but not the scale or mail, is unclear.

Dimensions of some examples of Roman scale armour						
Site	Period	Scale width	Scale height	Size ratio	Material	Type
Ham Hill	Roman (1st)	14mm	25mm	1:1.72	ae	regular
Corbridge	Roman (1st)	8mm	16mm	1:2.00	ae	regular
Usk	Roman (1st)	3mm	7mm	1:2.33	ae	hybrid
Ouddorp	Roman (1st)	6.5mm	11mm	1:1.69	ae	hybrid
Newstead	Roman (2nd)	13mm	29mm	1:2.23	ae	regular
Newstead	Roman (2nd)	7mm	10mm	1:1.43	ae	hybrid
Corbridge	Roman (2nd)	6mm	22mm	1:3.66	ae	semi-rigid
Mušov	Roman (2nd)	8mm	23mm	1:2.88	ae	semi-rigid
Cífer	Roman (2nd)	7mm	24mm	1:3.43	ae	semi-rigid
Carnuntum	Roman (2nd/3rd)	18mm	34mm	1:1.88	fe	regular
Carnuntum	Roman (2nd/3rd)	18mm	36mm	1:2	fe	regular
Carnuntum	Roman (2nd/3rd)	34mm	68mm	1:2	fe	semi-rigid
Carlisle	Roman (2nd)	16–22mm	44mm	1:2–2.75	fe/ae	semi-rigid
Carlisle	Roman (2nd)	18–24mm	54–62mm	1:2.58–3	fe/ae	semi-rigid
Carlisle	Roman (2nd)	12mm	24mm	1:2	fe/ae	regular
Carpow	Roman (3rd)	13–14mm	15–16mm	1:1.14–1.50	fe/ae	regular
Dura-Europos	Roman (3rd)	25mm	35mm	1:1.40	ae	horse armour
Dura-Europos	Roman (3rd)	45mm	60mm	1:1.33	fe	horse armour
Dura-Europos	Roman (3rd)	15mm	30mm	1:2	ae	cuisse
Dura-Europos	Roman (3rd)	45mm	60mm	1:1.33	fe	cuisse
Bizye	Roman (?)	6mm	12mm	1:2	ae	hybrid
Augsburg	Roman (?)	7mm	10mm	1:1.43	ae	hybrid

LAMELLAR ARMOUR

Like scale armour, lamellar armour derived its defensive strength from overlapped component scales (*lamellae*) but, unlike scale, the *lamellae* overlapped upwards. Each lamellar scale was partially covered by its neighbour directly below it and in turn partly covered the one above it. Similarly, it was overlapped by its neighbour to one side as well as overlapping its neighbour on the other side. It also differed from scale in that no twists of wire were used to join the *lamellae*, but rather a system of lacing was employed. This lacing was in part visible and not concealed, another point of difference from scale armour.

Lamellar armour does not appear to have enjoyed widespread use in the West during the Roman period, despite the presence of a number of units of Eastern origin. Some of the items identified as *lamellae* by Robinson (1975: 162) were in fact pieces from semi-rigid scale armour. Lamellar armour is not depicted in the iconographic sources and is absent from the archaeological record in the West.

History
Lamellar armour, like scale, is first recorded from Bronze Age Egypt (Dawson 2013: 61). In Europe, it is depicted in Etruscan art, such as the copper-alloy statue of Mars from near Todi (Italy), dating to the late 5th or early 4th century BC. The finely depicted cuirass has shoulder guards with what appear to be terminal rivet plates (and no central fastener), while there is a clear opening under the arm, on the wearer's left-hand side, with three pairs of disc-headed rivets shown. The cuirass is worn with *pteryges* at the bottom (but not at the arm openings), possibly from a padded garment beneath the

A relief from Palmyra showing the deities Aglibol, Baalshamin and Malakbel equipped with Roman swords worn over lamellar armour. The form of the swords suggests a 1st century BC date for the piece. (Photo Rama/Wikimedia CC-BY-SA 3.0 FR)

armour. This figure is close to life-size and bears an inscription on one of the *pteryges* in Etruscan characters but in the Umbrian language. A terracotta figure of a warrior from the pediment of the Temple of Apollo at Orvieto (Italy) shows a similar, if simplified, version of lamellar armour.

Where the Etruscans obtained the idea of lamellar armour is unknown. It does not seem to have been from the Greeks, the source of much of their military equipment, but equally they do not appear to have passed it on to the Romans once they were finally conquered in the 3rd century BC. The Roman re-acquaintance with lamellar armour came from the East, almost certainly in the first instance from the Parthians (who were by origin a steppe people). Indeed, it is in Scythian and Sarmatian cultural contexts that much of the early European evidence for lamellar armour can be found.

A relief from Palmyra (Syria), heavily influenced by contact with both Rome and Parthia, shows a triad of deities (Aglibol, Baalshamin and Malakbel) equipped with an eclectic blend of Roman weaponry and Parthian lamellar armour and it is not the only example of such sculpture. In a Roman context, a funerary relief from Kadıköy (Turkey), belonging to Severius Acceptus of *legio VIII Augusta*, depicts what some have interpreted as a padded garment, but may equally be a stylized representation of a lamellar cuirass. Actual finds of Roman-period lamellar armour are rare, however, the excavations at Dura-Europos producing parts of two leather cuisses (James 2004: 113 & 122–25) that are a variant on traditional lamellar armour that actually overlaps downwards, rather than upwards. Dura-Europos was also the source of a graffito of a *clibanarius* (a heavily armoured, lance-wielding cavalryman) that may also include lamellar armour worn around the abdomen, along with a composite set of plate and mail body and limb armour.

It was once thought that Roman-era lamellar armour was among the finds from the Thracian tumulus at Čatalka (Bulgaria). Re-examination, however,

Tombstone of the legionary Severius Acceptus depicting what might be either an arming doublet or possibly a cuirass of lamellar armour. (Drawing © M.C. Bishop)

Graffito from Dura-Europos depicting a *clibanarius* (it is unknown whether a Roman or a Parthian warrior is intended). The cavalryman may be wearing lamellar armour around his lower torso, while his mount is clad in a scale trapper similar to excavated examples from the site. (Photo Yale University Art Gallery)

has now shown this to be a hybrid armour made of plate and scale, almost certainly a form with Asiatic steppe origins (Negin & D'Amato 2018: 8).

Finally, although Robinson suggested that there were copper-alloy *lamellae* from Corbridge (1975: 162, Fig. 174), he had in fact misidentified individual *squamae* of regular semi-rigid scale armour, of which there are many more complete sections of similar shape and size (both published and unpublished), still articulated and complete with wire twists, from the site. Nevertheless, the myth of the Corbridge *lamellae* persists in modern works on Roman armour.

Although this apparent absence of archaeological evidence might cast doubt on the use of lamellar armour by the Roman Army before the Byzantine period, the circumstances of deposition and the materials used may have had an important bearing upon survival.

Description
True lamellar armour consisted of rows of overlapping metal or organic plates laced to their neighbours horizontally, then each row laced to its neighbours vertically, normally overlapping from bottom to top (unlike scale), although there are exceptions to this (as with the examples from Dura-Europos). As with scale, the edges of the defence could be bound in leather.

Variants
The absence of examples of lamellar armour from Roman contexts makes it very difficult to assess the range of forms of *lamellae* employed or to comment on any diachronic development there may have been. Just as

lorica segmentata may be suspected of being over-represented and mail under-represented in the archaeological record for depositional and other reasons, there must inevitably be a suspicion that lamellar armour suffers from a similar bias. It is also possible that historically differential degrees of archaeological research between the eastern and western halves of the Roman Empire may have something to do with the paucity of available archaeological evidence. It may be that in due course, as was the case with *lorica segmentata* from the Near East, increasing amounts of research on Roman military sites in the region may mean that examples of lamellar armour will come to light in the future.

There are two panels of a hybrid form of leather lamellar armour from Dura-Europos (James 2004: 122–25), usually said to be cuisses for the protection of the thighs of mounted troops, although it has been suggested that they are derived from horse armour (Dawson 2013: 71). James (2004: 123) noted that the pieces are more like scale than true lamellar, not least because they appear to overlap downwards rather than upwards. Both were found in Tower 19 along with other Roman arms and armour. The outer and inner faces have been determined by the use of the hair (or grain) side outermost on the *lamellae*, or inwards in the case of the lacing.

The first defence is 740mm long and 570mm wide, with its rectangular *lamellae* arranged in 13 rows. Most of these *lamellae* measure 40–45mm wide and 65–70mm high and are 3–5mm thick, but there is a bottom row that is larger, at 60mm by 90mm. A narrow leather lace runs horizontally along the front of each row of *lamellae*, while the rows are joined vertically to the rear by broader, red-dyed, vertical laces that are looped through each element to engage the horizontal lace to the front. In the bottom row, larger *lamellae* are joined horizontally by two narrow laces along the front, at both the top and the bottom of the row. The whole piece is edged in red leather and shows some signs of repair. One possible lace for attachment survives at the edge.

The second defence measures 660mm by 450mm and is composed of 12 rows of rectangular, black leather *lamellae* 40–45mm wide and 55–60mm

Remains of leather 'lamellar' cuisses from Dura-Europos showing front (left) and back (right) views. (Photo © Simon James)

Copper-alloy scale cuisse from Dura-Europos with textile backing and fragments of leather edging. (Photo Yale University Art Gallery)

high with a narrow leather lace running horizontally along each row and a broader one, dyed red, running vertically and, again, looped through each *lamella* to engage the horizontal lace. Five separate laces survive at the edges that may have served to attach the piece to a rider's leg.

MANUFACTURE AND DECORATION

Workshops

The available literary, epigraphic and archaeological evidence indicates that most arms and armour were produced by the Roman Army itself under the Principate. Justinian's *Digest* of Roman law included a passage attributed to the jurist and Praetorian Prefect Tarrutienus Paternus, recording the sorts of specialists within the legions, which included coppersmiths and blacksmiths (*Digest* 50.6.7). This is confirmed by a passage in the Late Roman epitomator, Vegetius, which is thought to have been taken from writings of the 1st-century AD military historian (and experienced military commander) Julius Frontinus, in which it was recorded that legions produced everything they needed themselves and that 'they even had workshops for shields, cuirasses, and bows, in which they fashioned arrows, missiles, helmets, and all sorts of weapons' (*DRM* 2.11). There were specific *fabricae* under the Dominate, many in or near military bases (as well as cities), in both the eastern and western halves of the Roman Empire, to produce the various types of military equipment (*Notitia Dignitatum*, *Or.* 11; *Occ.* 9). An inscription from Gaul shows cuirass manufacturers under the control of the Roman Army near Lugdunum (modern-day Lyon, France):

> For Marcus Ulpius Avitus, centurion of the *legiones III Augusta* and *IIII Flaviae* [and ...], the cuirass manufacturers (*opifices loricarii*) who existed among the Aedui and the settlement of Briva Sugnutia (Brèves) and those present under his command, out of respect for him, gave [this], well deserved (*CIL* XIII, 2828)

The inscription probably dates to the 2nd century AD, since one of Avitus' antecedents was evidently awarded Roman citizenship under Trajan. That is not to say that there was no private production of cuirasses for those who could afford to spend a little extra. A papyrus letter (*P. Giss.* 47) from an unknown individual to Apollonios, a local governor (*strategos*) in Egypt, dating to the second decade of the 2nd century AD, recorded the price of a brass cuirass as 360 *drachmae* (equivalent to around 90 *denarii*). The anonymous correspondent evidently viewed it as a bargain ('the cuirass – made of beautiful brass and of very fine construction, and very light weight in relation to its size, so that its wearer does not tire – would be respected by many'), and presumably it was offered by a private craftsman working in Koptos. To give some context, a Roman legionary at that time would have earned 300 *denarii* per annum.

Manufacture

The manufacture of mail required the smallest range of components out of any of the varieties of armour used by the Romans. A combination of solid and riveted rings was all that was necessary, together with fasteners (either hooks or breastplates) where the form of cuirass required it, and leather for edging, where needed. Solid rings could be made by welding wire or stamping plate, the former producing a circular cross-section to a ring, the latter rectangular, while riveted rings were also made from wire. To make the wire, ferrous rod would be pulled through a drawplate (of the same or harder material than the wire) with a series of gradually diminishing apertures (Sim and Kaminski 2012: 114–16). This process did not necessitate heating and each pass through would produce a wire of greater length and smaller diameter until the desired thickness was reached. Sheet metal, from which stamped rings could be made, was formed from ingots, either by beating or possibly by rolling (*ibid.*: 49–56). The techniques remained the same, regardless of whether copper-alloy or iron was the metal of choice.

Intriguingly, detailed examination of some mail from Zemplín (Slovakia) has suggested that at least some of the wire used to make rings for *lorica hamata* was made by forming tubes from sheet metal that were then passed through the drawplate (a process that has been termed roll-drawing), effectively coiling the sheet as this was done. Multiple passes through successively narrowing holes resulted in a tightly coiled structure in the wire that was visible when rings were examined microscopically (Özşen & Willer 2016). This may be the reason why some rings in mail shirts, such as that from Enns, have the appearance of being hollow once corroded.

Once the wire for riveted (and some solid) rings had been produced, it would have been wound around a circular-sectioned bar acting as a former to make a coil and then cut to form the individual rings. Wijnhoven (2021) has shown that Roman wire was almost invariably wound clockwise to form

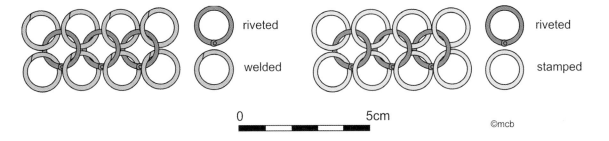

Types of rings used in Roman mail armour. (Drawing © M.C. Bishop)

rings, in contrast to the medieval period when an anticlockwise wind was favoured. This is then demonstrated in the archaeological record by Roman riveted rings always overlapping in a clockwise fashion. Once the wound wire was cut longitudinally, that intended for riveted rings needed to have its terminals flattened and punched to receive a rivet, as well as having the diameter slightly reduced in order to permit the overlapping holes to align (Wijnhoven 2021: 32).

Solid rings could be formed by simply welding butted rings once cut (and flattened slightly with a tap of the hammer, since they were cut from a coil). Stamped rings, on the other hand, required punches and corresponding dies to produce rings from sheet metal, with the internal hole punched first, followed by an external punch to produce a larger-than-desired ring, which would then be hammered down to its intended diameter on a mandrel, a process that produced slight faceting on the outer edge of the ring (Sim and Kaminski 2012: 123–28). Pairs of copper-alloy mail hooks to fasten the shoulder guards to the breast would have been cast using the lost wax method, since reusable two-part moulds were not adopted by the Roman Army until the 2nd century AD (Bishop & Coulston 2006: 243).

Production of the rings was only part of the process of producing mail, however, for assembly was required to make a functional defence. The basic tubular shape to cover the torso was simple enough, as were smaller, shorter sleeves for the arms. Both the area of the breast and the back could be continued upward in truncated rows, but the skill then lay in joining the trunk section to the sleeves. Part of the finishing process would have been to attach leather edging around all exposed edges (the bottom, arm openings and neck).

Evidence from the Vimose mail shirt shows that that defence at least was produced as one large, flat component that was then doubled over and joined at the sides with additional rings (Wijnhoven 2015b: 91). Reconstruction of a large fragment of damaged mail from the legionary fortress of Novae on the Danube River in northern Bulgaria not only enabled two original edges or hems to be identified, but also showed that one of these edges had an unusual diagonal step in it, only two rows deep (Wijnhoven 2015a).

Not all mail shirts were created equal, so the answers to questions such as 'how much did a mail shirt weigh?' and 'how many rings were there?' depend upon many variables. First, there was the diameter of the rings used and, in tandem with the diameter of wire employed, the aspect ratio between the inner and outer diameters. This would determine the number of rings over a given area. Since solid rings (whether welded or stamped) would be lighter than riveted rings, that difference – although miniscule between rings – would inevitably be significant when tens of thousands were combined to form a cuirass. The material used was also important: iron (7,850kg/

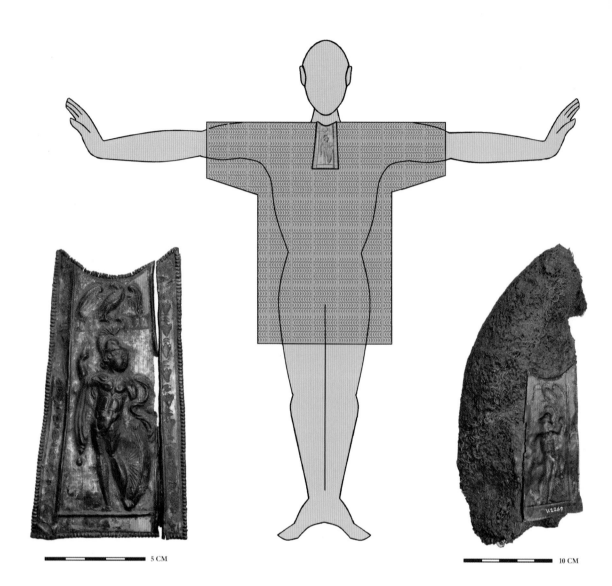

5 CM   10 CM

Reconstruction of the grid-pattern-decorated Bertoldsheim mail armour with details of the embossed and tinned central fastening plate of copper alloy (bottom left) and an overall view of the mail and plate (bottom right). (Photos and drawing © Martijn Wijnhoven)

m³) is lighter than brass (8,587kg/m³: Wijnhoven et al. 2021: 112). This is further complicated by the decision, in some instances, to use more than one metal for decorative effect, as was the case with the mail from Bertoldsheim. All of this means that mail defences could differ widely between individual cuirasses, with computer reconstruction indicating that the mail from Carlingwark Loch (Scotland) has been calculated as averaging 63,011 rings and 7.7kg, while that from Künzing (Germany) was 58,929 rings and 12.2kg respectively and Stari Jankovci (Croatia) 20,472 rings and 27.7kg (*ibid.*: Fig. 9). Finally, mail shirts may have varied in size according to the physical needs of the individual (although this need not necessarily have been the case, since military forces throughout history have sometimes exhibited a one-size-fits-all policy).

Sim and Kaminski (2012: 132) conclude that a mail shirt made of 6mm-diameter rings would require around 40,000 rings and that production of both the riveted and solid rings would require a total of 200 man-days, with assembly requiring an additional 30 man-days. Of course, there was always scope for delegating elements of the manufacturing process among

A ferrous wire drawplate found at Vindolanda. (Photo © The Vindolanda Trust)

both skilled (i.e. the craftsmen) and semi-skilled workers (ordinary soldiers after some brief instruction, for example), so that those 230 man-days need not have taken anything like 230 calendar days.

To make the metal components of scale, both sheet metal (for the scales themselves) and wire (for the twists) were needed, and these could be of copper alloy or iron. Although Roman depictions often show scales as having a medial vertical ridge, in reality this is an extremely rare feature among archaeological finds, although it can be found on the scales used on hybrid armour. Once cut out, scales had to be punched with the requisite number of holes, according to their function, the punching process leaving a small burr around the hole on the reverse face (these burrs actually have an important part to play in the articulation of the cuirass). Scales were often flat, like some of those from Carnuntum, but occasionally slightly convex, as with the Newstead scales. Wire for the twists had to be drawn in exactly the same way as that for the rings of mail and then cut into short lengths to facilitate this process.

Just as with mail, production of the components probably preceded assembly, simply because that would be a more efficient way of managing the task of producing a cuirass. Rows of scales could be built up and then passed on for attachment to a foundation garment. The construction of scale was more complex than mail insofar as more than one type of scale was necessary to construct a cuirass, whereas only two types of ring were needed for mail. Nevertheless, by experimentation, Sim and Kaminski (2012: 104–08) were able to reduce the time needed to produce one scale from sheet metal to between 1.5 and 3 minutes, according to the method of production chosen. The number of scales in a defence obviously depended upon the size of the individual scales employed, but might vary between those with larger scales and those with smaller scales.

In reconstructing hybrid mail and scale armour, for which both the sizes of the rings and the scales are much smaller than their regular equivalents, Schmid (2009: 67) suggested that a mail shirt with an estimated 160,000 rings and 20,000 scales would require 500 man-days for completion. Brass mail from Xanten, with an average ring density of 305,426/m², may well have belonged to such composite armour (Wijnhoven et al. 2021: Fig. 9).

The production of a semi-rigid cuirass was slightly different to that of regular scale, since rows had to be wired to each other rather than sewn to a garment. As with mail, scale was finished off with leather edging in the manner of the Carpow cuirass, although such edging also seems to be shown in some of the iconography.

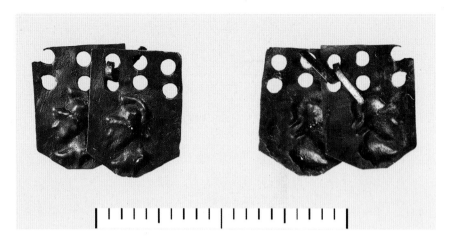

The question of whether wrought iron or steel was used for Roman armour is as relevant for mail and scale as it is for plate armour (Bishop 2022: 48). There are inherent difficulties in studying Roman mail, however, not least because so little of it survives and, when it does, it is often heavily corroded, more often than not into a solid mass. Examination (combined with experimentation) does suggest that rings were made of iron but work-hardened, because of the way in which the rings were formed (Sim and Kaminski 2012: 132–33). On the other hand, metallographic examination of some of the scales from Carlisle revealed that they had undergone one-sided carburization (so that the inner face was iron but the outer was higher in carbon and thus steel), but it is not certain how this effect was achieved (*ibid.*: 165–66) or whether it was intentional.

Decoration

Mail armour made of ferrous rings could incorporate decoration by using copper-alloy rings to form a pattern. The manufacturer of a cuirass from Bertoldsheim used this technique to produce a grid pattern, and a set of copper-alloy rings from Vechten (Netherlands) has been interpreted as deriving from the edge of a sleeve opening (Wijnhoven 2017).

Scale could also be decorated, most commonly with copper-alloy scales alternately tinned, effectively producing a chequerboard pattern (as with those from Ham Hill). A patch of scale still attached to its breastplate used ferrous and copper-alloy plates to achieve a decorative pattern, as did the neck segment from Carlisle, with its single vertical column of brass scales within an otherwise ferrous cuirass. Another set of ferrous scales from Carlisle had separate, thin copper-alloy scales attached over the front of the main scales in a similar alternating pattern. These additional scales simply utilized the standard twists of wire by means of which the main scales were joined laterally, but this was an unusual practice. Examples of copper-alloy scales have also been found embossed with the head of Minerva, the Roman goddess of wisdom, although to date no examples are known from stratified contexts.

The hybrid mail and scale armour from Bizye seems to have had a more ambitious decorative scheme. The main body of the defence was made up of copper-alloy scales on a base of copper-alloy mail with an arrangement of ferrous and silvered copper-alloy scales forming a double row of rhombuses around the base of the armour and on the shoulder guards.

Copper-alloy scale armour found in the Iron Age hillfort of Ham Hill. (Photo © J.C.N. Coulston)

Both mail and scale could be fitted with embossed, decorated breastplates to assist with the putting on and taking off of a defence. These have long been interpreted as belonging to 'parade' armour but it is now clear that they in fact belonged with functional battle armour (Bishop 2022: 32–34). Legionary inscriptions incorporated into the decorative schemes confirm the use of both mail and scale within legions during the 2nd and 3rd centuries AD, and breastplates from Carlisle belonging to scale and one from Bertoldsheim belonging to mail illustrate the function of such plates.

Maintenance

Such is the integrity of mail armour that, unlike *lorica segmentata* (Bishop 2022: 51), it is seldom found in the archaeological record. It usually occurs as a few connected rings, or occasionally as complete cuirasses, as at South Shields, Künzing and Zugmantel. Even when damaged quite severely, a mail shirt would not necessarily fall apart as readily as segmental armour. Moreover, the 'self-cleaning' action of the rings on their neighbours whenever the wearer moved ensured that the development of corrosion was unlikely in everyday use. Even if left unattended for a while (as the examples in the Carnuntum *Waffenmagazin* seem to have been), repeated subsequent wearing would tend to remove light corrosion through abrasion and restore the cuirass to its original condition. If damage did occur (as the direct

Two fragments of standard (flexible), ferrous scale armour from the Carnuntum *Waffenmagazin*. (Photo © Andreas Pangerl)

49

Reconstruction of copper-alloy scale armour showing damage to individual *squamae* caused by everyday wear. (Photo © J.C.N. Coulston)

result of receiving a blow from a hand-held weapon or a missile strike, for example) it could easily be repaired by means of the substitution of some replacement rings.

Scale armour, on the other hand, was not so easily maintained (Croom 2000: 132). Since they were made of fairly thin sheet metal, scales were vulnerable to damage at the exposed edges. Combat damage requiring replacement would also require any affected scales to be detached from both their neighbours and from the underlying garment. Reconstructed semi-rigid scale has shown that this form was also at risk of damage from over-articulation, when it was flexed beyond the limits afforded by the amount of movement available from the wire twists joining the scales, and that everyday use could also take its toll on scales damaged by contact with other equipment (such as belts or scabbards) in a soldier's panoply (Croom 2000: 130).

 CLEANING LATE ROMAN ARMOUR

Maintenance of equipment was as much of a necessary task in the Dominate period as it was earlier. In an echo of earlier times (Bishop 2022, Pl. C), Dominate-era *limitanei* of *legio II Augusta*, now based in the shore fort at Rutupiae (modern-day Richborough, England), take advantage of fine weather on the south-east coast of Britannia for some cleaning and maintenance of both mail and scale body armour, sitting outside on wooden stools. One man (**1**) is recommissioning a neglected ferrous mail shirt, which is both corroded and damaged as a result of some past skirmish. A repair to a damaged section near the hem is visible as an area of bright, uncorroded rings as he concentrates on replacing a few rings in a much smaller area of damage. He has a bucket with dry sand nearby in which he will agitate the mail and clean it mechanically, once he has finished repairing it. Strips of tanned leather lie next to him ready to repair the edging of the mail once it has been cleaned.

Another man (**2**) is attending to replacing damaged brass scales on an otherwise gleaming cuirass, stitching each replacement to the fabric backing and then wiring it to its neighbour on either side. Other men are cleaning helmets and one (**3**) is attending to a leather shield cover, patching tears and replacing damaged stitching.

The Carnuntum *Waffenmagazin*

At the end of the 19th and beginning of the 20th centuries, serious archaeological excavations began on the legionary fortress at Carnuntum (near Bad Deutsch-Altenburg, Austria). As part of his examination, the Austro-Hungarian artillery officer, Maximillian von Groller-Mildensee uncovered a building full of Roman military equipment of various types and which he termed the *Waffenmagazin* (or 'weapons store', possibly an *armamentarium*). The *Waffenmagazin* was 15m wide and 33m long and was part of a rampart-back structure, incorporating Buildings IV to VI, which was 100m long. Building VI formed the southern portion with seven rooms, five of them (rooms i, k, l, m and n) arranged around a central massive core, while room g (11.45m by 8–9m) was the only one with underfloor heating and may have been an office associated with the store. The western rooms (i and m) were at ground level, while the others were some 1.4m higher with steps between them. Room h (11.45m by between 2.8m and 3.85m), located between the office and store rooms themselves, was interpreted as a handling area. Room i (2.6m by 7.5m) evidently contained arrows and shields, room l (4m by 7m) spears, room m (2.5m by 7m) helmets and '*lorica segmentata*' and room k (3.3m by 3.8m) a selection of items.

In all, Groller noted 121 pieces of scale armour (both large and small); 302 of '*lorica segmentata*'; two fragments of mail and 14 of what he called *Drahtpanzer* ('wire armour': probably a misinterpretation of heavily corroded mail); ten of armguards; 62 of shields (mostly bosses); one bronze humeral (as he termed it); 58 pieces of helmet; 13 from swords; five from daggers; 38 from shafted weapons like spears; 11 *pilum* fragments; 40 spear butts; 209 arrowheads; and 166 miscellaneous items (which clearly included pieces of composite bows, among other things). This made a grand total of 1,052 pieces (Groller 1901a: 41–44).

The sheer amount (and wide range) of material found enabled Groller to illustrate plate, mail and scale armour, there being so many examples of the last that he developed a typology based upon their peripheral holes for attachment in order better to understand the variants. He concluded that the assemblage was composed of nine basic types to which scales of all shapes and sizes conformed.

The whole building had burnt down, possibly in the 2nd century AD, the iron artefacts that fell to the floor as the shelving collapsed quickly forming a 'layer of rust' that preserved the wooden uprights of the shelving and mineralized some of the organic components (such as traces of wood, leather and textile).

Unlike mail, hybrid mail and scale appears to have been more vulnerable to attrition, presumably because the wire used for the rings, whether it be of copper alloy or ferrous, was so much finer. By the same token, finds of individual scales from this form of armour are extremely rare. This means it is very difficult to judge how common this form of defence was, since it is unclear whether it was very common but not very vulnerable (as with regular ferrous mail) or less common but more prone to damage. Such are the vagaries of the archaeological record.

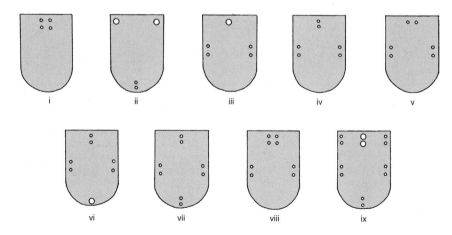

The principal types of Roman scales identified by Groller from among the Carnuntum *Waffenmagazin* finds. (Drawing © M.C. Bishop)

MAIL AND SCALE ARMOUR IN USE

Understanding how all Roman armour was used has been greatly aided by the plethora of reconstructions based on archaeological evidence that followed on from Robinson's pioneering work, although, as with all experimental archaeology, they can only ever show what was possible, not what actually happened. That said, the overall fragility of segmental body armour in comparison to mail seems beyond doubt, and the archaeological evidence clearly indicates that the evolution of segmental armour was guided by pragmatic responses to genuine problems that arose from its use. It is not for the modern commentator to decry *lorica segmentata* as a flawed form of defence when the Romans seemed quite happy to rely on it in battle for more than 300 years.

Combat

The continued use of plate, mail and scale into the Late Roman period serves to demonstrate that, to the Romans at least, there was no one perfect form of body armour. Sim and Kaminski outlined a series of compromises that had to be made for mail, scale and plate concerning weight, the amount of protection afforded and ease of manufacture (2003/4: 95, Table 11). Their conclusions may perhaps be modified to allow for the relative proportions of the three main types of armour surviving (and recognized) in the archaeological record. It might also be suggested that durability was worst for segmental armour (finds of which are common), best for mail (which is rare and even then possibly biased towards complete cuirasses), and somewhere in between

Roman legionaries and a cavalryman in combat with Parthians, depicted in relief on the bowl of a cavalry helmet found in the burial at Tell Oum Hauran. Here, mail appears to be indicated with a regular pattern of dots while scale is shown with wavy horizontal lines. (Drawing © M.C. Bishop)

for scale. Hybrid mail and scale armour may have been more vulnerable than both mail and scale and thus disproportionately represented among finds, but there is no real way of verifying this assertion. Modern experimental archaeology and scientific analysis can confirm or refute such impressions by exploring the strengths and weaknesses of the respective types.

In combat, both mail and scale faced two main types of blow that they had to counter: the edge and the point – effectively blunt- and sharp-force trauma. The first might come from the blade of a sword (or, in extreme cases, the scythe-like *falx* used by Thracian warriors), while the second could be a stabbing blow resulting from a thrust or even a missile strike from a javelin, arrow, or slingshot. The energy dissipation characteristics of both mail and scale worked in their favour against an edged weapon, although they were perhaps more vulnerable to a point, whether it was from a sword, spear, or arrowhead.

Detailed, published scientific studies of the effects of different weapons on mail and scale are sadly few and far between, although various more-or-less rigorous experiments are recorded on social media. Unfortunately, many of these are flawed in their methodology and are thus of comparatively little value, although the work of Edelson (2007) on replica medieval mail armour is of more interest than many. He found that mail could resist penetration by bodkin-headed arrows shot from a 70lb draw-weight bow down to a distance of *c*.4.5m.

The wire ties of semi-rigid scale served to hinder sword or spear thrusts upwards under the scales, something to which the Masada and even Ham Hill scale armour cuirasses would have been vulnerable. It is particularly noteworthy that a reconstruction of one of the Carlisle sets of semi-rigid armour was able to resist a bodkin-headed arrow shot from a 50kg-draw-weight longbow at a distance of just 1m from the armour. Overarm blows with both sword and axe were similarly ineffective, largely due to the overlapping of the scales producing a stepped effect that spread the force of the blow (Sim & Kaminski 2003/4: 44–47).

Carriage

Modern-day Roman re-enactors have long known that by far the easiest way to don a one-piece mail shirt is to place it on a flat surface (a table or the ground, for instance), bend over and insert one's arms through the sleeves, then (with arms raised) stand upright and allow the defence to fall down the body and seat itself correctly. As such, this can be done in seconds, which cannot be said of plate armour or, so far as it is possible to tell, scale armour.

Regardless of the variant, mail places all of its weight upon the shoulders of the wearer. This can to some extent be alleviated by the wearing of a waist

G **CAVALRY PATROL**

A *turma* (squadron) of cavalry encounter some light resistance while patrolling on a native trackway through a field system in the territory of the Corieltauvi of Britannia. They wear a mixture of mail and scale with shoulder guards, while the *signifer* (standard-bearer; **1**) and *decurio* (cavalry officer; **2**) wear hybrid mail and scale with much finer *squamae*. The armour worn by junior officers could vary considerably, some featuring brass *squamae* with alternate scales tinned, while others used iron scales. Some of the ordinary troopers (**3, 4, 5**) wear regular scale armour of brass; again, this was sometimes decorated with alternating tinned scales. Other men (**6, 7**) are wearing leather-edged mail shirts with shoulder guards and prominent triangular gaps in the lower hem of the armour. All of the troopers would be wearing a short padded garment (*subarmalis*) beneath their armour. The harnesses of their horses pre-date the invasion of Britain, employing ring junctions and lobate pendants, while the men wear a diverse range of helmets characteristic of the cavalry.

belt (*balteus*), which transfers a proportion of the weight to the wearer's hips. Even so, wearing mail – the heaviest of the three principal types of body armour – for protracted periods can be fatiguing.

Scale was lighter but also cinched at the waist in order to reduce the burden upon the shoulders of the wearer. The evidence for a fabric foundation garment and the use of first shoulder guards and later breastplated openings might be thought to suggest that scale armour, like mail, was essentially tubular in form and donned in one piece. Semi-rigid scale, on the other hand, with much less 'give' in the cuirass, was presumably broken into front and rear portions, otherwise storing it when it was not being worn could have been fairly problematic.

The lamellar depicted on Etruscan warriors seems to have been fastened under the arms, so when it was worn in later periods it may well have been fastened in much the same way.

As was the case with plate body armour (Bishop 2022: 57), some form of padding underneath both mail and scale was essential for the successful operation of the armour. The anonymous Late Roman author of the *De Rebus Bellicis* called this type of garment a *thoracomachus* and medieval copies of the illustrations that accompanied the text show them displayed on posts with cross bars.

> Among all those things thought of in antiquity, anticipating its use in war, is likewise added the *thoracomachus*, astonishingly useful for relieving the weight and roughness of equipment for the body. For this kind of garment, which is made from felt to the measure and for the protection of the human torso, devised from soft wool with masterful

skill through fear and anxiety, so that the main cuirass, or *cliveanus*, or the like, would not injure the delicate body by its roughness or weight; moreover, limbs in the garment, aided by this comfort, can perform tasks amid the hazards of combat and winter. To be sure, in case this same *thoracomachus*, when subject to heavy rain, should be hampered by its weight, it will be advisable to cover it with well-finished Libyan skins following the form of that *thoracomachus*. (*De Rebus Bellicis* 15.1–3, tr. author)

Mail, by its very nature, dissipates some of the energy of a blow, but a padded undergarment (variously 'arming doublet' or '*subarmalis*' in modern literature) only helps further with this task, as well as bearing the brunt of the grime that inevitably accumulates when wearing armour. Such an undergarment, with a fringed hem, may well be depicted being worn under mail on some Rhineland tombstones from the 1st century AD, notably those of Firmus from Bonn and an unidentified soldier from Andernach. Having argued that mail was depicted using paint, Robinson nevertheless seems to have thought that the depiction of the fringes on these in fact represented mail worn under a cover. Padded undergarments may later have come to include *pteryges*, and this may well be what is shown in the relief decoration on one of the cavalry helmets from Tell Oum Hauran, where mail-clad legionaries with *pteryges* below and at the shoulders battle Parthian warriors.

Scale armour already had a foundation garment included as an essential part of its construction, to the point where it might be more correct to identify *lorica squamata* as an armoured garment (in some ways anticipating the medieval jack of plates or brigandine). An element of caution in accepting Groller's identification of straw attached to the linen underlying scale from the Carnuntum *Waffenmagazin* would not be amiss – it could have been a storage medium – but one interpretation of this finding could certainly be the use of straw as padding for the garment underlying the scales. The

 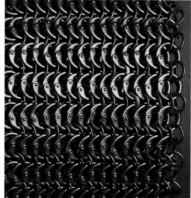 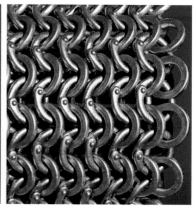

Computer reconstructions of Roman mail from Carlingwark Loch (left), Xanten (centre) and Künzing (right) used in determining 'stretchability', weight per m² and effective coverage of this type of armour. (Modelling © Aleksei Moskvin/ Sketchfab/CC-BY-SA 3.0)

scale-clad Sertorius brothers, on their tombstones from Verona, both had *pteryges*, although there is no way to know whether these were attached to the foundation garment or an additional, separate padded garment worn underneath the armour.

Versatility

A mail cuirass was every bit as flexible as *lorica segmentata* in that it imposed few restrictions upon bodily movement. Troops wearing it could just as easily march, work and fight while wearing it as their colleagues in plate body armour. Its main drawback came from fatigue induced by its weight, something that could be alleviated, if not completely mitigated, by cinching it with a belt over the hips. Although constructed of rigid rings, the amount of movement between neighbouring rings afforded the flexibility necessary for the cuirass. While it is difficult to measure this with physical examples of mail, computer modelling has been used to show the range of movement possible within Roman-era mail armour by quantifying the 'stretchability' (the difference between full compression and full extension in both the horizontal and vertical axes) of reconstructed sections of several mail shirts of different periods (Iron Age, Roman and post-Roman). Mail from Künzing, for example, dating to the 3rd century AD, had a stretchability of 34.2 per cent in the horizontal plane and 6.5 per cent in the vertical. This compares with 103 per cent and 27 per cent respectively for mail from Carlingwark Loch, and 4 per cent and 0.3 per cent for Late Roman mail from Stari Jankovci. The compromise here is that the greater the stretchability, the less the overall coverage – or, to put it another way, the bigger the gaps! This research has also shown how Roman mail was both lighter and more flexible than some at least of its Iron Age predecessors (Wijnhoven et al. 2021: 109–16).

Rear view of a reconstruction of semi-rigid scale. (Photo © J.C.N. Coulston)

Similarly, troops wearing scale armour had to be able to perform the same range of tasks, including the construction of fortifications, or it would have placed them at an undesirable disadvantage. The Carpow armour illustrates how a scale cuirass could be folded over, while mail naturally forms an amorphous blob when dropped onto a flat surface, although it is equally possible to roll or neatly

Standard-bearers and musicians depicted on Trajan's Column wearing mail armour. (Photo © J.C.N. Coulston)

fold it (Croom 2000: 129). Semi-rigid scale was much less flexible and modern reconstructions have highlighted the need to store it flat or hang it up (*ibid.*, 132). Nevertheless, the difference between the diameter of the wire ties used and the holes through which they passed would always mean that a degree of flexibility was retained, even if it was not as great as that of true scale sewn to a backing. This limited amount of movement will inevitably have affected the form of any cuirass made using this type of scale. Whereas regular scale, like mail, could be employed to cover the awkward angles of the shoulders and top of the arms to form rudimentary short sleeves, much as is shown on the Adamclisi metopes, semi-rigid scale could not be employed in this way as it would limit the degree to which the wearer's arms could be raised.

Who wore what?

The sculptors of Trajan's Column were very careful to create a codified system whereby troop types could be easily identified by onlookers. Citizen soldiers (legionaries and Praetorians) were depicted in *lorica segmentata*, auxiliary infantry and cavalry in mail, and exotic foreign troops in scale (the exceptions being legionary and Praetorian standard-bearers and musicians, both of which were shown in mail). Both near-contemporary tombstones (such as those of C. Castricius Victor and C. Valerius Crispus for mail and the Sertorius brothers for scale) and the Adamclisi metopes give the lie to this stereotyped uniformity and make it clear that both legionaries and auxiliaries could use mail and scale at this time. Moreover, both the representational and archaeological evidence confirm that the contemporaneous use of both mail and scale continued throughout the Principate and on into the Dominate.

Representations of Roman scale armour, particularly on tombstones, often show it with a central vertical ridge that, as has already been noted (see p. 46), seems primarily to have been a characteristic of hybrid mail and scale (and possibly one reason why this type of defence has been associated, rightly or wrongly, with the term '*lorica plumata*'). This might then suggest that what appears to be regular scale on the tombstones of junior officers was, in fact, intended to represent hybrid mail and scale. Such a suggestion is, of course, impossible to prove, but the possibility that the type of scale worn may have been a measure of status should at least be borne in mind.

Although the available evidence indicates that *lorica segmentata* was exclusively the preserve of citizen troops during the 1st and 2nd centuries AD (Bishop & Coulston 2006: 254–59; Bishop 2022: 60), it is all too clear that mail and scale were used by both legionaries and auxiliaries (infantry and cavalry) throughout the Principate and on into the Dominate.

Legacy

The Romans may have adopted mail from north-west European elites and found a way to make it common issue to their troops, but in so doing they ensured its transmission back to potential barbarian enemies as part of diplomacy, the arms trade and the acquisition of booty by those raiding the Roman Empire. The mail shirt from Vimose is a small part of this narrative (Wijnhoven 2015b), which essentially guaranteed that early medieval Europe would see mail continue in military use, uninterrupted. This cuirass shows many Roman elements, not least the clockwise winding of the wire used, but incorporates characteristics that are strongly suggestive of local manufacture or, at the very least, adaptation, in much the same way that Roman *spathae* were adapted (Bishop 2020b: 59–60).

A slightly different use of exported Roman mail seems to have occurred in the Przeworsk culture in what is now Poland. A series of finds from 2nd/3rd-century AD female burials included, among the grave goods, fragments of mail, often associated with small model shields similar to one carried by a Roman standard-bearer on a relief from Carrawburgh in England (Bishop 2020b: 42). These fragments of mail have been suggested as souvenirs or charms worn by women and made from Roman mail (Czarnecka 1994).

The transmission eastwards of mail to the Sassanid Persian empire is demonstrated by the armour from the Dura-Europos mine (see p. 20) and the rock-reliefs at Firuzabad (Iran) from the time of Ardashir I (r. AD 211/12–24), founder of the Sasanian Empire.

Mail is still with us: it can still be found used for protection by butchers (to prevent injury when chopping meat), glaziers (to assist in handling sheet glass) and divers (to protect from shark bites). The legacy of scale armour is by no means so certain, however. That scale armour was in use in the early medieval period is not in doubt, but it seems likely that its development among steppe peoples such as the Avars ran parallel to, rather than as a result of, that of Rome, and the same can doubtless be said of lamellar armour. Nevertheless, the concept of scale armour is far from dead. Dragon Skin body armour, formed from overlapping ceramic discs, was briefly evaluated in the early 21st century by the US Army and apparently found some use among special forces and bodyguards despite official disapproval, but this form of armour is still under active development in China (Chen 2022).

H **LEGIONARIES IN A DANUBIAN FORTRESS**

A *centuria* of legionaries is paraded outside its barrack block and its commander has started inspecting them at the leftmost *contubernium* (a unit composed of eight legionaries). The ordinary soldiers wear a mixture of mail and scale cuirasses, while the *centurio* wears a finer mail cuirass (with smaller rings) with shoulder guards. He is accompanied by the *signifer*, who has a wax tablet to take notes and is wearing a hybrid mail and scale cuirass with small ribbed scales and a decorative grid pattern of tinned scales (but no standard, helmet, or animal pelt, since he is fulfilling his clerical duties). Some of the men still wear the fringed *subarmalis* but others now have the newer version with *pteryges*.

BIBLIOGRAPHY

Ancient sources

CIL – *Corpus Inscriptionum Latinarum*. Epigraphik-Datenbank Clauss/Slaby. Available at https://tinyurl.com/ryexz6k

De Rebus Bellicis. Hassall & Ireland 1979.

Justinian, *Digest*. 1932 Central Trust Company ed., trans. S.P. Scott. Available at https://tinyurl.com/ybc66j2j

Notitia Dignitatum. Available at https://tinyurl.com/uvz3z4e

Paulus Orosius, *Historiae Adversum Paganos*. 1936, trans. I.W. Raymond. Available at https://tinyurl.com/bdhy6ywn

Polybios, *Histories*. 1922–27 Loeb ed., trans. W.R. Paton. Available at https://tinyurl.com/298bsf

Tacitus, *Annals and Histories*. 1925–37 Loeb ed., trans. J. Jackson. Available at https://tinyurl.com/8jpv49

Varro, *On the Latin Language*. 1938 Loeb ed., trans. R.G. Kent. Available at https://tinyurl.com/rhade6v

Vegetius, *De Re Militari*. 1885 Lang. Available at https://tinyurl.com/ybvq5ypu

Modern sources

Anon (2014). 'Caerleon exhibition shows horses' history in warfare', *South Wales Argus*, <https://www.southwalesargus.co.uk/news/11311768.caerleon-exhibition-shows-horsesrsquo-history-in-warfare/> Accessed 16.2.22.

Anstee, J.W. (1953). 'Fragments of Roman "bronze" scale armour from Corbridge', *Museums Journal* 53: 200–02.

Bishop, M.C. (2020a). *Roman Shields*. Elite 234. Oxford: Osprey.

Bishop, M.C. (2020b). *The Spatha: The Roman Long Sword*. Weapon 72. Oxford: Osprey.

Bishop, M.C. (2022). *Roman Plate Armour*. Elite 247. Oxford: Osprey.

Bishop, M.C. & Coulston, J.C.N. (2006). *Roman Military Equipment from the Punic Wars to the Fall of Rome*, ed.2, Oxford: Oxbow Books.

Cheben, I. & Ruttkay, M. (2010). 'Römische Militärausrüstungsgegenstände aus dem germanischen Grubenhaus in Cífer', *Slovenská Archeológia* 58.2: 309–36.

Chen, S. (2022). 'Fish scales inspire Chinese bulletproof vest resistant to armour-piercing rounds', *South China Morning Post* <https://www.scmp.com/news/china/science/article/3163461/fish-scales-inspire-chinese-bulletproof-vest-resistant-armour> Accessed 18.1.22.

Coulston, J.C.N. (1990). 'Later Roman armour, 3rd–6th centuries AD', *Journal of Roman Military Equipment Studies* 1: 139–60.

Coulston, J.C.N. (1999). 'Scale armour', in Dore, J.N. & Wilkes, J.J., 'Excavations directed by J.D. Leach and J.J. Wilkes on the site of a Roman fortress at Carpow, Perthshire, 1964–79', *Proceedings of the Society Antiquaries of Scotland* 129: 481–575.

Croom, A. (2000). 'The wear and tear of third century military equipment', *Journal of Roman Military Equipment Studies* 11: 129–34.

Croom, A.T. (2001). 'A ring mail shirt from South Shields Roman fort', *The Arbeia Journal* 6–7 (1997–98): 55–60.

Curle, J. (1911). *A Roman Frontier Post and its People. The Fort at Newstead*. Glasgow: Maclehose.

Czarnecka, K. (1994). 'The re-use of Roman military equipment in barbarian contexts. A chain-mail souvenir?', *Journal of Roman Military Equipment Studies* 5: 245–53.

D'Amato, R. & Negin, A.E. (2017). *Decorated Roman Armour: From the Age of the Kings to the Death of Justinian the Great*. Barnsley: Frontline Books.

Dawson, T. (2013). *Armour Never Wearies. Scale and Lamellar Armour in the West, from the Bronze Age to the 19th Century*, Stroud: Spellmount.

Edelson, M (2007). 'Riveted maille and padded jack tests', *myArmoury.com Discussion Forums*, posted 12.9.07 <http://myarmoury.com/talk/viewtopic.php?t=11131> Accessed 15.12.21.

Gilmour, B.J. (1999). 'The mail shirt', in Niblett, R., *The Excavation of a Ceremonial Site at Folly Lane, Verulamium*, Britannia Monograph Series 14, London: Roman Society: 159–67.

Greiner, B.A. (2008). *Rainau-Buch II. Der römische Kastellvicus von Rainau-Buch (Ostalbkreis)*, Theiss: Stuttgart.

Groller, M. von (1901a). 'Das Lager von Carnuntum', *Der Römischer Limes in Österreich* 2: 15–84.

Groller, M. von (1901b). 'Römische Waffen', *Der Römischer Limes in Österreich* 2: 85–132.

Hansen, L. (2003). *Die Panzerung der Kelten. Eine diachrone und interkulturelle Untersuchung eisenzeitlicher Rüstungen*, Kiel: Hansadruck.

Hassall, M.W.C. & Ireland, R., eds (1979). *Aspects of De Rebus Bellicis*, BAR International Series 63, Oxford: BAR.

Howard-Davis, C. (2009). *The Carlisle Millennium Project: Excavations in Carlisle, 1998–2001, Volume 2*, Lancaster imprints 15, Lancaster: Oxford Archaeology North.

James, S. (2004). *The Excavations at Dura-Europos: Conducted by Yale University and the French Academy of Inscriptions and Letters. VII, The Arms and Armour and Other Military Equipment.* London: British Museum.

Kelly, F. & Schwabe, R. (1931). *A Short History of Costume & Armour, Volume 1, 1066–1485*, London: Batsford.

Lipsius, J. (1630). *De Militia Romana Libri Quinque, Commentarius Ad Polybium*, Antwerp: Officina Plantiniana.

Müller, F. (1986). 'Das Fragment eines keltischen Kettenpanzers von Tiefenau bei Bern', *Archäologie der Schweiz* 9: 116–23.

Negin, A. & D'Amato, R. (2018). *Roman Heavy Cavalry (1): Cataphractarii & Clibanarii, 1st Century BC–5th Century AD.* Elite 225. Oxford: Osprey.

Özşen, I. & Willer, F. (2016). 'Gezogener antiker Draht? Zur Drahtproduktion des Kettenpanzers aus Zemplín', *Restaurierung und Archäologie* 9: 85–102.

Robinson, H.R. (1975). *The Armour of Imperial Rome.* London: Arms & Armour Press.

Rose, W. (1906–08). 'Römisch-germanische Panzerhemden (Altertum – Zeitalter der Völkerwanderungen – Frühes Mittelalter bis zur Karolingerzeit)', *Zeitschrift für historische Waffen- und Kostümkunde: Organ des Vereins für Historische Waffenkunde* 4, 1–8, 40–55.

Schmid, E.D. (2009). 'Details of lorica hamata squamataque manufacture', *Journal of the Mail Research Society* 2.1: 67–76.

Sim, D. & Kaminski, J. (2003/04). 'Lorica squamata: the production and testing of scale armour from the Carlisle Hoard', *Journal of Roman Military Equipment Studies* 14/15: 41–48.

Sim, D. & Kaminski, J. (2012). *Roman Imperial Armour: the Production of Early Imperial Military Armour*, Oxford: Oxbow Books.

Vujović, M. (2015). 'Ring mail from Galerius' Burial Rite at Gamzigrad (Romuliana)', in Vujović, M., ed., *Ante Portam Auream: Studia in Honorem Professoris Aleksandar Jovanović*, Belgrade: University of Belgrade: pp. 239–50.

Wijnhoven, M. (2009a). 'Lorica hamata squamataque: a study of Roman hybrid feathered armour', *Journal of the Mail Research Society* 2:1: 3–29.

Wijnhoven, M. (2009b). 'The Ouddorp lorica: A case study of Roman lorica hamata squamataque', *Journal of the Mail Research Society* 2:1: 30–50.

Wijnhoven, M. (2022). *European Mail Armour. Ringed Battle Shirts from the Iron Age, Roman Period and Early Middle Ages*, Amsterdam Archaeological Studies 29. Amsterdam: AUP.

Wijnhoven, M.A. (2015a). 'Filling in the Gaps: Conservation and Reconstruction of Archaeological Mail Armour', *Journal of Conservation and Museum Studies* 13(1), p.Art. 8.

Wijnhoven, M.A. (2015b). 'The iron tunic from Vimose (Funen, Denmark): further research into the construction of mail garments', *Gladius* 35: 77–104.

Wijnhoven, M.A. (2017). 'A very Roman practice: copper-alloy decoration in mail garments', *Journal of Roman Military Equipment Studies* 18: 183–96.

Wijnhoven, M.A. (2021). 'Clockwise or anti-clockwise? A method for distinguishing Roman from medieval mail armour', in Hoss, S., ed., *The Production of Military Equipment – Fabricae, Private Production and More*, Panel 9.1, Heidelberg: Propylaeum: pp. 25–46.

Wijnhoven, M.A., Moskvin, A. & Moskvina, M. (2021). 'Testing archaeological mail armour in a virtual environment: 3rd century BC to 10th century AD', *Journal of Cultural Heritage* 48: 106–18.

Wild, J. (1981). 'A find of Roman scale armour from Carpow', *Britannia* 12: 305–06.

INDEX

References to illustrations are shown in **bold**. Plates are shown with page locators in parentheses.